TRAUMAS AND TANKS

FOR JOHNNY

Do not despair
For Johnny head in air.
He sleeps as sound
As Johnny underground.
Fetch out no shroud
For Johnny in the cloud,
And keep your tears
For him in after years.
Better by far
For Johnny the bright star,
To keep your head
And see his children fed.

John Pudney
(As featured in the film
The Way to the Stars)

TRAUMAS AND TANKS

A Child's War

written and illustrated by

TONY GARNETT

First published in the United Kingdom in 2009
by The Hobnob Press, PO Box 1838, East Knoyle, Salisbury, SP3 6FA
www.hobnobpress.co.uk

Text and illustrations © Tony Garnett, 2009

The Author hereby asserts his moral rights to be identified as the Author of the Work.

All rights reserved. No part of this publication may be reproduced, stored in a retrieval system, or transmitted in any form or by any means, electronic, mechanical, photocopying, recording or otherwise, without the prior permission of the publisher and copyright holder.

British Library Cataloguing in Publication Data
A catalogue record for this book is available from the British Library

ISBN 978-1-906978-09-9

Typeset in Chaparral Pro 12/15pt, with headings in Gill Sans.
Typesetting and origination by John Chandler
Printed by Lightning Source

Contents

Illustrations   7
Dramatis Personae   9

1	Father goes to war	11
2	Air-raid precautions	15
3	A hollow tree and a barrage balloon	21
4	The mumps and a gas practice	26
5	A frozen field and a wicked nanny	30
6	New neighbours and a birthday party	38
7	Uncle John's farm	47
8	A broken leg and Annie goes missing	56
9	Hetty Brake and a gashed head	67
10	Aunt Ellie and a tea-time ritual	75
11	The camp, hospital and a German bomber	81
12	A drowning, an accident and a fatal illness	90
13	Brian encounters a tank and loses his parents	101
14	Toboggan rides and trains in the attic	114
15	An airfield encounter and unwelcome news	123
16	Peace at last	128

Illustrations

1. *Father says good-bye to the family* — 13
2. *The hollow elm tree* — 20
3. *Tim tries on his gas-mask* — 29
4. *Marie steals apples in the attic* — 36
5. *The Mason boys meet the Keelings* — 43
6. *A German fighter over Uncle's farm* — 54
7. *Brian is caught in the bombed building* — 62
8. *The boys chat to wounded Americans* — 85
9. *Tim and Hugh discover a dead body* — 94
10. *Grandpa is killed by a train* — 97
11. *The boys observe the hearse from upstairs* — 99
12. *Brian's bicycle is crushed by a tank* — 105
13. *A glider makes a forced landing* — 108
14. *A flying bomb destroys the Royal Oak* — 112
15. *Mr Moore's toboggan sets off at speed* — 117
16. *The boys play with trains in the attic* — 121

Dramatis Personae

The MASON family
Mr Harold Mason
Mrs Mary Mason
Chris, Tim and Annie

The KEELING family
  (next-door neighbours)
Maj. Leslie Keeling RAMC
Mrs Dorothy Keeling
David, Peter and Sheila

The BORRODAILE family
  (at the bottom of the road)
Mr Borrodaile
Mrs Borrodaile
Michael and Helen

Mr Tillman (local farmer)
Hugh (his son)

The MOORE family
  (owners of the garage)
Mr Jack Moore
Mrs Moore
John (Chris's friend)

The COMBER family
Mr John Comber (a farmer, and the Mason children's uncle)
Mrs Beth Comber
Angela and Trudy

Brian Priddy (Tim's friend)
Mr Harracott (milkman)
Bill Hardiman (Uncle John's foreman)
Marie O'Brien and Hetty Brake (nannies)
Mrs Johnson (driver of YMCA van)
Philip (her son)

I
FATHER GOES TO WAR

There was tension in the air; it was almost palpable. Sitting on the stairs in the middle of the night, Tim Mason knew instinctively that this was going to be an unusual day. In the chill air of the bedroom he had huffed at the frost patterns on the inside of the window and scratched a small area clear with his finger-nail so that he could peer out. But there was nothing to see, merely a pitch-black darkness; not a glimmer of light was showing in the town. Only the gentle soughing of a bitterly cold east wind could be heard as it forced its way through the ill-fitting panes of glass.

'Come down, dear,' called his mother. Tim could sense the strain in her voice. He wondered what might be the cause of it.

It was on the third step from the top that Tim sat every morning, the frayed edges of the stair-carpet pressing through his thin pyjama bottoms, his feet tickled by the rough sisal material. At this spot, at exactly the right height, a knot in the wooden panelling that boxed in the staircase had fallen out, forming a perfectly round hole. By this means, as through a fish-eye lens, Tim could spy out the goings-on in the kitchen below.

'Come on down, dear, please. I know you're there. And call Chris, will you? Make sure you've got your dressing-gowns on – the boiler's gone out again and it's very cold down here.' His mother's voice sounded fretful, pitched higher than usual. She walked round the kitchen, filling the kettle and putting it on the gas with little Annie in her arms. Annie sucked her thumb and made murmuring noises.

Clearly this was not a normal day. Tim had been disturbed during the night by muffled thumps and bangs coming from his father's bedroom, which was next to the room he shared with his brother, and light had kept falling across the landing floor from his father's half-open door. Tim had more than once sat up, disturbing the old mother cat who slept at the end of the bed, keeping his feet warm. She yawned, stretched out her paws and waited for him to settle down again.

From the bathroom down below came the rhythmic back and forth of a razor being sharpened on its leather strap, the sounds of running water and washing, and then steps once more on the staircase. Waking again, with a start, Tim had caught a glimpse of his father on the landing in his heavy khaki greatcoat and carrying a large kitbag.

At last, Chris, Tim's elder brother by three years, appeared at the top of the stairs yawning ostentatiously. 'What's all the fuss about? Why have I been woken up? It's the middle of the night, for God's sake!' Chris knew exactly what was going on, having been told earlier by his mother, but loved a bit of drama. If he could add to the tension, and if he was in that sort of mood, then he certainly would. He knew his father was a scientist attached to the Meteorology Department of the War Office and was going out to serve in the Far Fast.

'Be quiet, Chris, and try and be a bit more helpful,' scolded his mother. 'Tim, dear, your father's going overseas to help with the war and will be gone a long time. We don't know when we'll see him again.' These last few words were forced out from behind a handkerchief which she was holding to her nose.

There was a knock at the front door; a shadowy figure could be seen dimly through the glass panels. Father and Mother embraced briefly and little Annie was kissed on the top of her head. Chris's earlier bravado was deserting him now: he was fond of his father, and as the first-born had shared in the happier years of his parents' marriage. Each son was hugged in turn as Father said, 'Be good to your mother. Help her as much as you can – and no fighting, all right? I'll write when I can.' He opened the door and joined his driver outside as his kitbag and briefcase were taken to the waiting car. The door closed. The silence that followed was broken only by a stifled sob from their mother, and the sound of the car engine outside receding into the night.

The dispirited group shuffled back into the kitchen, the boys wandering what to do and how to deal with the emotional atmosphere. Mrs Mason said decisively, 'Well, let's all go to bed and try and get some sleep.'

1. Father says good-bye to the family

She went back to her downstairs bedroom, where she slept with little Annie, who was still in a cot, beside her. The boys returned upstairs, where Chris made a sort of hurrumphing sound as he rolled over and faced the wall. Tim stroked the cat and settled her down as best he could but, turning over the extraordinary events in his mind, he found that sleep was impossible. Now that their father was gone who would play cricket in the garden with them at weekends or help mend their bikes? But at least there would be no more of those terrible rows that occurred so frequently. Nearly every evening after finishing his meal Father would say, 'I'll just pop out and buy some cigarettes. I won't be long.'

Mother would protest, knowing that he would only be back after the pubs had closed. The boys upstairs would listen to the angry exchanges, the slamming of doors and their mother's sobs – which tore at Tim's heart.

Mother cat purred as he climbed back into bed, making dough on the eiderdown with her claws. Tim rubbed her behind her ears, thinking that at least some things in the household were loving and dependable. An early rising cockerel crowed from a garden further down the street, while the whistle of a steam engine and the distant clanking of coal wagons being shunted heralded the start of another wartime winter's day.

2
AIR-RAID PRECAUTIONS

By then in its third year, the war had become for everyone a tedious time of make-do and mend, of scrimping and saving, of ration books and annoying shortages. And just as with so many other families whose fathers were away on active service, the task of running the home had fallen firmly on Mother's shoulders.

How different it had been during those grim days of 1940 when England had seemed to be at the mercy of the enemy poised just over the Channel. It was clear that Hitler was preparing for an invasion and first needed to clear the skies of British fighters. When he failed in this he bombed the airfields, and finally, in desperation and fury, he turned on our towns and cities.

While Father was still at home he was there to take decisions; as master of the house he held the children's attention and respect. One dark winter's day, as Sunday dinner was about to be put on the table, he waved everyone to their seats and said sternly, 'Now be quiet! I want to listen to the one o'clock news. You know that Germany has been battering London every night for weeks now? Well, the bombers are closer to us now: they've been raiding Southampton and Portsmouth for the last few nights. Even poor old Salisbury has had a few stray bombs. Lord knows who'll be next!'

Their mother laughed. 'Young Desmond at Southampton was on fire duty one night when a bomb landed in the River Itchen and blew all the salmon up into the branches of nearby trees. The locals had a bonanza. Perhaps every cloud *does* have a silver lining!'

The boys smiled but watched their father, who was clearly not amused at her levity. They had more sense than to interrupt or offer their own views; Father was intolerant of their opinions. They were in awe of him, since he rarely hugged or cuddled them; that would be too unmanly. He often barked unkindly, so when he was in the house they learned to keep their distance and gauge his mood. Their hearts would leap when he said, 'Well, let's go into the garden for some cricket, shall we? You look as though you could do with some fresh air. Chris, get the gear, and Tim, put on some plimsolls. Look lively now!'

Chris would react immediately. 'Good old Dad,' he would think to himself. Tim was more cautious, since his father was something of an enigma to him, and often to be avoided especially when he was in a temper. While Chris seemed to have a more natural rapport with him, Tim rarely felt comfortable in his company. His mother would smile and say 'I don't think your father understands you at all' as she pulled him close for a cuddle. Then Tim would relax and feel a warm glow inside.

But today, after Sunday lunch, the familiar and fixed routine was being played out. Total quiet was demanded while their father listened to *ITMA*. Tim heard brief snatches from the wireless as he sat finishing a puzzle in the sitting room. There was the inevitable shout of laughter when the office cleaner asked, 'Shall I do you now, Sir?'

It was 'quiet time' in the sitting room. Chris was busy stitching the background of a large woolly rug, the interesting part, a bird design, already completed. Similarly Tim had got to the boring part of his puzzle, and was filling in the sky behind a range of mountains. Their mother's knitting needles kept up a steady staccato clicking as yet another grey jersey took shape on her lap; while little Annie helped to ball up the wool until one of the kittens got it into a complete tangle. Their father was by now settled in the armchair, and his daughter wheedled to be allowed to climb onto his lap for a cuddle. Gloating over this enviable position, Annie smirked at the two boys and then sniffed loudly at his waistcoat, saying 'pooh' in exaggerated disgust at the smell of stale tobacco smoke. Her father smiled indulgently and eased her down onto the floor after a few minutes, so that he could concentrate on the *Sunday Times*.

Slowly the newspaper slipped from his fingers and slid from his lap onto the floor. A gentle snoring started, followed by louder grunts and snorts which rattled his false teeth. At this Tim started to snigger while his mother smiled. Chris slipped quietly out of the room, returning after a few moments with a feather which he waved back and forth under his father's nose. The eddies of air caused it to twitch and made him sneeze.

'Careful,' said Mother. 'Don't you dare wake him up. There'll be the very devil to pay!' Chris returned to his rug-making and Tim to his puzzle: the monotony of a winter's Sunday afternoon dragged interminably on.

'They'll be delivering the Morrison shelter later in the week,' said Father at tea. 'Lucky, really.' The town had been hit already – not as a deliberate target, but by pilots who had lost their way or had offloaded their bombs in panic.

'Yes,' said Mother. 'Do you remember last summer when that stick of bombs fell near John's farm? The craters they left filled with water and kids used them as swimming pools. And worst of all, the wretched bomber terrified the farmer's pedigree Jerseys. They were scattered in all directions, and it took hours to round them up.'

'The shelter had better go in your bedroom downstairs, and the two boys must come down and sleep with you. Better to be safe than sorry. It'll probably be for only a few weeks.'

The two boys looked at each other and back to their mother. 'At least we won't be traipsing out into the cold during the night like those poor people with Anderson shelters in their gardens,' she said with feeling. Tim wasn't sure of the difference but decided not to ask.

'Well, I'd better get ready for air-raid duty,' said Father, as Mother cast a strained look in his direction.

'But I thought you clocked on at ten.'

'Yes, normally, but we've things to sort out beforehand.' He avoided looking in her direction.

'Things that are best discussed at the King's Head? Why can't you stay in for a bit and do something with the children? They never see you during the week.'

He made for the stairs without replying. His wife knew by now how restricted he felt by his home and family: unlike many other men he did not seem to be fulfilled by watching them develop and grow. His spirit seemed to need some greater, though undefined, freedom in which to flourish.

The family relaxed once he had gone, and Tim decided to do some piano practice. He had not been learning very long and was struggling with a simple Mozart minuet transcribed for children. The mistakes came thick and fast.

'What an awful row,' groaned Chris. 'Can't you put a sock in it? There's a good Biggles book here. Why don't you read that and give us all some peace.'

Tim choked back a tear and returned to his puzzle. Chris, on his way to the kitchen, bumped into the table by accident and knocked some pieces onto the floor.

'Now look what you've gone and done, you blundering oaf. I'll tell Mum of you.'

'I think I'd better get some supper,' she said in an attempt to calm things down. 'What about beans on toast?'

'God, not shirt-lifters again,' groaned Chris, mainly to show off his latest grown-up expression. 'Tim will stink the bedroom out tonight. Perhaps I'd better wear my gas-mask.'

Their mother laughed, and peace descended once more. As Annie was taken off to bed Tim suggested they should play trains. This was rather childish for Chris but he agreed, and together they started to rearrange the sitting-room furniture. The sofa and two armchairs were pushed into an arc, their arms touching to make narrow tunnels underneath. Two upright chairs were tipped onto their fronts with their backs overlapping. The giant world atlas made a bridge across to a table, and a rug was thrown over the whole makeshift contraption to complete a trackway within a darkened tunnel. On all fours the two boys thundered round and round, weaving in and out of the obstacle course, their hands and feet drumming on the carpet, their sweating bodies crashing into each other. Mother cat, disturbed by all the commotion, cried by the door to be let out.

Eventually the game palled and the hot, weary boys went upstairs to get ready for bed. Their nightly visit to the freezing cold bathroom had been honed to a fine art: a quick splash of water on the face, a dab under each armpit, then back up the stairs in double-quick time.

'I'm keeping my vest and socks on,' giggled Tim. 'You're just a filthy little toad,' sneered Chris. 'No girl will ever want to have anything to do with you.'

Tim pondered these words in the dark of the night, and wondered why Chris felt it necessary to be so unkind.

2. *The hollow elm tree*

3
A HOLLOW TREE AND A BARRAGE BALLOON

'Whoopee,' thought Tim as he sat up in bed. 'It's Saturday again!' Mother cat stirred, yawned at this unwelcome disturbance, and went back to sleep again. The sun shone through the crack between the curtains, casting bright semicircular shapes on the ceiling above. Daringly Tim shied his teddy bear at Chris, who muttered, 'Stop it, you silly twit,' rolled over and went back to sleep.

The start of the weekend was such an exciting time after the routine of school days, so full of anticipation and promise. Tim felt a surge of joy as he struggled into his old shirt, corduroy trousers and short-sleeved jersey. Without lingering on the stairs he sat down for breakfast and was soon joined by his brother.

'Let's grab our bikes and go down the lane. The others are bound to be there,' Chris suggested.

Tim agreed. 'But we'd better watch out for thorns – we don't want punctures again like last week.'

'Can I come too?' asked Annie.

'Don't be daft, you're much too young,' shouted Chris, dragging his bike out of the shed.

Annie started wailing as his mother shouted after him, 'There's no need to be so unpleasant to your little sister, is there?'

Four years younger than Tim, Annie soon quietened down and smiled broadly when her mother suggested they did some cooking. 'Ooh, yes, let's.'

'We'll make some scones for tea, shall we? Put your apron on, dear, and I'll get the flour.'

The boys freewheeled down the hill, scuffing their shoes along the road to act as brakes. They pulled up next to the partially hollow and very old elm tree at the corner of the lane. This magnificent giant of a tree had been struck by lightning many years earlier, but after losing its top half still retained its lower sturdy branches, ideally spaced for the children of the area to climb.

Already there were two boys high up in the tree. Chris jumped for the lowest branch and swung himself up, monkey-like, to join them. Tim went round the side to where a knotted rope had been hung to help the smaller boys get started. He manoeuvred carefully until he was level with a hole in the trunk where a branch had been ripped off. From inside there came a dreadful raspberry, imitating a long drawn out animal fart. It could only have come from the notorious Brian Priddy, always up to mischief, always at the centre of any trouble.

'What the devil was that dreadful noise in aid of, you stupid twerp?' shouted Tim angrily.

Down below a small knot of girls had gathered. Zoë Warren and Helen Borrodaile cast sidelong glances at the older boys and whispered to each other. The boys pretended not to notice, but Chris broke off twigs and bombed them from above. The girls squealed and pretended to resent the attention. Brian Priddy, having struggled out of the hollow section of the tree, merely gobbed down on them, with surprising accuracy. At this they drifted away, muttering, 'Filthy blighter, he's so disgusting – I hate him.'

'See who can get to the end of the hedge without touching the ground.' Michael Borrodaile threw down the challenge, which was eagerly taken up by Chris and John Moore, his best friend. They extracted themselves from the branches of the elm tree and levered themselves onto the thorn and beech hedge that stretched along the lane. The younger boys followed as best they could. This hedge had grown out of control and acted as a windbreak for the allotments on one side. While the original top of the hedge provided a firm foothold, the upper untrimmed branches allowed the boys to swing their way along from hand to hand.

The thorns tore at their jackets and corduroy jerkins but the material was tough, and like a group of chattering monkeys they struggled their way along. Soon the younger boys were left far behind and started grizzling.

A rhythmic scrunching of thick tyres on the gravelly, muddy lane and the sound of a lorry engine made Tim turn his head. A moment later a large army truck pulled alongside and a khaki-capped head poked out through the window.

'Wotcher, kids. Having fun? Seen any other lorries or soldiers down this lane? We took a wrong turning in town and got separated from our mates. They should be somewhere round here.' Tim shrugged his shoulders and looked vacant.

'What's the problem? Cat got your tongue, has, it?' laughed the driver.

Brian Priddy responded rudely, 'If we'd seen any blooming soldiers around here we'd have told you, wouldn't we? But we haven't so we can't, OK?'

'Well you're a cheeky little bleeder,' said the driver, winding up his window and engaging gear.

Tim cast his eye over this strange vehicle as it passed slowly by. Behind the cab was a large wire-framed cage with a winch inside it and a heavy cable. Next to that a tarpaulin concealed a bulky shapeless object heavily tied down with ropes, and behind the double rear wheels the lorry towed a trailer full of neatly stacked gas cylinders. Was this the gas that their parents were always going on about and which caused such anxiety? It all seemed to be under control, and did not look to Tim like one of Hitler's fearsome weapons of war.

The older boys had already spotted other vehicles and soldiers near the cowsheds at the end of the lane, and directed the driver towards them. As the lorry passed, Chris nudged John Moore. He had spotted a corner of the tarpaulin being lifted and the half-hidden face of Brian Priddy leering out from underneath.

'Get walking, you suckers!' he shouted, giving them all 'V' signs. The tarpaulin dropped back into place.

'My God! He's really done it this time,' muttered Chris in disbelief.

Everyone was getting hungry by now so they decided to break off for dinner, and arranged to meet later to find out what was going on.

✳ ✳ ✳

When the boys re-assembled they found that a gate had been opened into the field near the cowsheds, to allow more vehicles through. The lorry with the winch was at the centre of a crowd of soldiers, some very busy and others standing about aimlessly. From time to time they fed a heavy cable from the winch, which was driven by power from the lorry's engine. Others struggled to control an enormous floppy bag that lay heaving on the grass. There seemed to be a continual shouting of orders, and at times even laughter. Of Brian Priddy there was no sign.

Tim asked Colin Braithwaite, 'What are they going to do with that great big silver bag?'

'Don't you know what a barrage balloon is?' Colin replied, surprised at his younger friend's ignorance. 'They're putting them up to protect the railway yards just over the river. They think the bombers may go for the railways after they've finished with the ports.' Colin had been the first to arrive, and had gleaned this information from one of the soldiers. He was not going to pass up the opportunity to show off his newly acquired knowledge. 'We've got to keep well back in case the cable breaks.'

The gas bottles had been connected now, and the floppy bag kept rising up in billowing jerks. First it looked like a sackful of fighting ferrets, then like a small whale, and finally like a cheerful cartoon elephant swaying from side to side just off the ground. The men watched as it rose steadily higher into the sky, its silver skin reflecting the sun in blinding flashes as it twisted and turned, straining hard at its moorings.

'Won't the bombers see the balloon and avoid it?' asked Tim, still rather bewildered.

Colin thought for a few moments. 'Well it'll go much higher.' He paused. 'And at night they won't be able to see it anyway.' A further pause followed as he remembered what he had been told. 'Of course it's the cable that actually knocks the plane down – it tears their wings off.'

The afternoon wore on, and by tea-time the soldiers had finished their training. The balloon, bucking and pitching against the gusts of wind, was slowly winched down and, accompanied by breathy wheezes and belches of gaseous air, was deflated and stowed under its tarpaulin. Leaving a guard to watch over it, the soldiers piled into a covered wagon and left the field to the crows and rabbits.

Rushing into the kitchen, Tim blurted out to his father, 'You'll never guess what we've seen today. They're putting up a barrage balloon in the field at the end of the lane. It's fantastic. They say it's there to protect the railway lines.'

His father was reading the newspaper and hardly looked up. 'Yes, we've known about that for weeks. Now us poor air-raid wardens will have even more to check up on every night.' Crestfallen, Tim left the kitchen and slowly went upstairs.

'Do you always have to be such a killjoy?' Mother wearily chided. 'He was so looking forward to telling someone about his discovery.'

Her husband looked up, nonplussed. Shaking his head, he folded the newspaper carefully and put it in his pocket. He looked at his watch and said, 'Well, I must pop out and buy some cigarettes.'

Yet another long evening stretched ahead.

4
THE MUMPS AND A GAS PRACTICE

'I've got a sore throat and my neck hurts,' announced Tim one morning, feeling sorry for himself.

Mrs Mason tried to gloss over this remark as she got on with the breakfast. 'Let's feel your forehead. Oh dear, you're burning up. You'd better go back to bed. No school for you today. I'll come in and see you later.'

By now, during these more dangerous months of the war in which there was an increased risk of air-raids, the children were sleeping in their mother's large bedroom downstairs. Their father still slept upstairs – but he was often out at night on his air-raid warden duties. Tim crept back inside the Morrison shelter, which was designed to protect the occupants of a house from falling timbers and masonry. Chris's bed was on top; little Annie shared her mother's bed.

Tim lay on his back, idly wiping his finger on the condensation of the cold reinforced ironwork. He touched his neck; it felt spongy, very hot and quite painful. Why did he feel so ill? Was he going to die? He embarked upon a flight of fancy, imagining his shocked friends, the stillness in the house, the muffled voices. Would he find out what Heaven was like? With this thought he drifted off into a fitful, dream-filled sleep.

A hearty banging on the front door woke him suddenly. 'Well, where is the little whipper-snapper? Gone to join the angels yet?' A booming Scots accent filled the house as Mother pushed open the bedroom door. Things never seemed so bad once the doctor had arrived. 'Good Lord, you look as snug as a bug in a rug tucked up in there. Sit yourself up so I can take a good look at you.' The doctor pushed a thermometer under Tim's tongue while running a stethoscope over his chest and back. He glanced towards the large bed. 'What, not my beautiful little Annie as well? We'd better check her over too.'

For the first time Tim noticed his sister in bed as well. He must have been asleep for hours.

The doctor wiped the thermometer clean and said, 'We'd better not risk her mouth. Tim, close your eyes and face the wall.' He winked at their mother and rolled Annie onto her front, pulling up her nightie and gently inserting the thermometer. 'Yes, her temperature's up as well, but you'll both live.' He laughed cheerfully. 'It's the dreaded mumps, I'm afraid. There is a lot of it about. You'll feel pretty sore for a few days, and with that throat of yours, Tim, there'll be no scrunchy fried bread for you, just lots to drink and sloppy bread and butter pudding to eat. You'll like that, won't you!'

Tim pulled a wry face, and they all smiled.

With the doctor gone, the bedroom became a sick-room for the next few days. Chris joined them too, also poorly. 'Well, at least I'll miss school,' he said, until it was pointed out that since it was Thursday it would mostly be the weekend he was going to miss. Soon there were cold meals half-eaten on bedside tables and drinks spilled on bedcovers. From time to time their mother threw open the windows to air the room, which sent the boys burrowing deep under the bedclothes.

One evening, as quiet settled on the house for the night, they were woken by muffled footsteps outside. Suddenly the bedroom door was thrown open and a ghastly reptilian figure with rubber head and enormous eyes appeared. A powerful torch beam swept round the room and over the half-asleep children. Annie, terrified, burst into tears; Tim, mostly through sheer surprise, joined her. Only Chris kept his head, shouting out, 'It's only Dad in a gas-mask,' adding, after a moment, 'I can't think what all the fuss is about.'

Their mother was beside herself with anger. 'What in God's name did you do that for?' she scolded, gathering up Annie and Tim in her arms. 'This is an air-raid drill,' her husband answered in a voice of authority. 'There are enemy aircraft about and there could be a gas attack. We've been told to make it as real as possible to see how well people are prepared. You'd better get into your gas-masks at once.'

'What an absolutely ridiculous idea,' said his wife angrily. 'Now Chris has gone down with mumps they're all three ill.' And, glancing at her husband meaningfully, she added ruefully, 'God knows how we're going to pay Dr Burkett's bill.' Her comment was left hanging in the air as their father abruptly left the bedroom.

Tim settled back into bed as best he could and listened to the sounds of the night. There was a muffled banging of doors and the sudden sweep of torch beams out in the street. He could hear the sound of aeroplanes overhead – the enemy, recognisable by the unpleasant rasping noise made by their engines: they were left unsynchronised to increase the agitation of the people listening in fear below.

The mention of gas-masks reminded him of the moment some weeks earlier when their father had piled four boxes on the kitchen table. The boys, intrigued, had pulled out curious rubber masks with large eye-pieces and protruding circular 'noses'. They were vivid blue and red and soon acquired the name of Mickey Mouse masks. Chris yanked his roughly over his head and made mooing noises as he danced round the house, shouting, 'Look, Mum, I'm a heffalump!'

Annie just looked nervous and sucked her thumb.

Tim peered through the goggles, repelled by the mask's vile rubber smell. He soon tore it off.

'Come on, Mum. Try yours on. It's bigger than ours and it's black. And where's Annie's? It must be in this box we haven't opened yet.'

What appeared from inside the last box caused immediate consternation. It was a complicated rubbery bag with an inner and outer layer, a wide plastic eye-piece and built-in respirator. Annie resisted as she was laid on the table and the hood was pulled over her head. She struggled and squirmed and punched the sides with her fists, her face turning red and then almost purple behind the plastic window. She was fast becoming hysterical, and there was nothing her mother could do to calm her down. 'Dear God, let's hope we never have to use these in earnest,' she said in exasperation as she released the screaming child.

3. Tim tries on his gas-mask

5
A FROZEN FIELD AND A WICKED NANNY

'The blasted boiler's gone out again,' grumbled Mother, as she lit the gas and put the kettle on. 'The coal we've been getting since the war started is absolute rubbish.' She returned to the bathroom and took off her pyjama top ready to start washing. The singing of the kettle brought her back into the kitchen.

'Morning, Mrs Mason. And a fine frosty one it is, too.' A tall gentleman in a rough tweed jacket was sitting near the open door rolling a cigarette. He raised his battered trilby hat as the lady of the house fled half-naked from the room, taking the hot kettle with her. As he slid his tongue along the cigarette paper his Adam's apple moved up and down under his collarless shirt.

'I'm sorry, Mr Harracott, I forgot it was Saturday. I'll just fetch the milk money for you. Harold went off abroad during the night so we're all at sixes and sevens today.'

'Oh, did he now?' replied the milkman without much interest, as he slipped the coins into a worn leather bag. 'Things are going to be a bit tricky for you now,' he muttered as he wandered out.

'Silly old curmudgeon,' she thought, smiling.

Tim listened to this exchange as he pulled back the bedroom curtains. With the immediate danger of bombing now past, the two boys had forsaken the discomfort of the Morrison shelter and returned to their upstairs bedroom. He looked at the icy rime under his finger-nails as he scratched at the frost-covered windows and shivered at the sight of the white hoar covering the privet hedge in front of the house. Two housewives with shopping bags were going up the road to the little grocer's on the corner, their shoes sounding strangely loud on the hard-frozen pavements.

Tim watched Mr Harracott climb onto his milk-cart and slap his horse's back with the reins to persuade him to move on up the hill. He often went out to see the horse and give him a dry crust of bread or some oats, but today he was too late. He watched his mother talk to the postman.

'Only one for you today, Mrs Mason. Husband gone yet?'

'Yes, he went last night with his friend Freddie. The first few days are the really worrying ones – through the Channel and the Bay of Biscay. They should be all right after that.'

'Are they going the long way round?' asked the postman sympathetically.

'No, through the Med. They're dropping off aircraft fitters at Malta, then more troop reinforcements for Auchinlech at Alexandria, then on to India through the Canal. Mind you, I shouldn't really be telling you all this: I could get myself shot!'

She laughed as the postman said, 'Well, don't worry yourself too much. The next thing is you'll be getting a letter describing the fleshpots of Egypt, and knowing how the Army works there'll probably be ten all at the same time.'

'I'm sure you're right, but it's something else to worry about in this damn war.'

After their unexpected lie-in Chris and Tim were anxious to make up for lost time. Over a late breakfast their mother told them that she had been offered some piano teaching that afternoon, and had asked Marie, the Irish girl, to keep an eye on them for the afternoon.

'God, not her,' groaned Chris. 'You know she pinches things from the larder.'

'Well, I'm not sure about that. And anyway she's a poor unfortunate girl who's been unkindly treated by the world. And,' she added almost as an afterthought, 'she's free this afternoon.'

Tim grumbled as they went out to fetch their bikes. 'Nasty creature. Her teeth are yellow. And I suppose she'll bring that awful baby with her, stinking the place out with its poo!'

At the hollow elm tree they were told that most of the others were down by the river where the fields had flooded. They hurried off down the lane, their tyres skidding as they broke through the frozen puddles, mud and water splashing their trousers.

'I can hear them but where are they?' Tim shouted out in excitement.

Chris stood up on his pedals and craned his neck over the hedge. 'There,' he pointed. 'Behind the cowsheds.'

A group of boys and a few girls were standing round a large impromptu ice-rink: after a long period of very low temperatures, the flooded field had frozen solid. The braver boys were running hard across the grass, launching themselves onto a slide that stretched, like the runway of an airfield, across the longest span of ice. Bodies flew in all directions, with arms and legs windmilling wildly as their owners struggled to remain upright. Casualties limped off clutching at bruised limbs.

Chris fell spectacularly and banged his head, but maintained a brave and stoical silence. Mick and Peter McLean collided, and fell sprawling into a watery patch where the weak sun had caused the ice to melt. Jerkins and trousers were soaked and legs became cold, wet and uncomfortable – but this in no way spoiled their fun.

Although some eventually wandered off home in ones and twos to get warm, the rest turned towards the river to seek out more sport. They threw stones at the moorhens, and watched their feet spinning frantically as they skittered across the water. Some climbed willow trees on the river-bank, but the old wood was friable and the branches split off easily.

Brian Priddy, it had to be him, disturbed two swans sheltering in the reeds. Finding a long stick, he proceeded to molest them, seemingly oblivious to the hissing of the cob as it reared up to protect its mate. Only when it flapped its enormous wings and advanced aggressively towards him did he retreat and join the others, who were already hiding behind tree-trunks.

Getting bored at last, and also very hungry, they turned for home. As they cycled past the Borrodailes' house Helen called out to ask if they were coming to her ninth birthday party that weekend. Tim slowed down to have a chat with her, but Chris, knowing she had a childish crush on him, rode scornfully past.

✳ ✳ ✳

'Well, what did you do this morning?' asked their mother as she dolloped large helpings of mashed potato onto their plates with a wooden spoon and covered it with a thin gruelly mince and cabbage from the garden. The boys tucked in hungrily. 'You haven't answered my question. I can see your clothes are soaking wet, so you've obviously been up to something. You'd better put dry things on straight after dinner. And Chris, make sure you keep an eye on little Annie until Marie comes, will you? Oh, yes, we're short of apples. Can you bring some more down from the attic while I'm out, please.'

'Anything else you'd like me to do while you're gone?' asked Chris in a sarcastic tone of voice. 'Re-decorate my bedroom? Do next week's ironing? Take the cat to be neutered?'

'Now don't be difficult, dear. Just do as you're asked and fetch the apples.'

Chris loped upstairs two at a time with the attic key, a candle and some matches. Tim followed hesitantly with an old shopping bag. If his elder brother was going into the fearsome attic then he would be brave enough to follow, but to go into that dark cavernous space alone was quite out of the question. Because it was in there that the source of Tim's anxieties and the cause of his earliest nightmares was to be found.

The house, being a semi-bungalow, had two centrally placed upstairs bedrooms set in the roof, with a cramped and narrow triangular space running along each side. Although used mainly for storage, these two attics were kept locked since not all the floor had been boarded over. Patches on the kitchen ceiling showed where feet had slipped off the joists and burst through the lath and plaster. One attic housed the apple store.

Sometimes, but only when their mother was out, Chris and Tim ventured into these attics out of sheer devilment. Holding a candle and a box of matches, Chris's stooping figure would make its way deeper and deeper into the claustrophobic gloom, with Tim scrambling as close as possible behind him. Strange shapes and shadows would play across the walls as the dread built up steadily in his mind. What nameless beasts lurked in those dark corners? What unspeakable horrors did the shadows conceal? What apparitions might suddenly be realised in that ghastly alien space? At the precise moment that these fears were at their height Chris would blow out the candle and groan in a ghoulish manner. Tim would backtrack for all he was worth towards the light of the half-open door. In those early days floods of tears would inevitably follow: 'I'll tell Mum of you.'

These childhood fears were not helped by Chris, who had poked a pencil through the plaster of the bedroom wall from inside the attic to make a series of holes – and had been known to make fearsome noises through these as Tim was trying to go to sleep. How could he ever be safe now that phantoms and spirits could seep unbidden into the bedroom at night?

'I'm not going in if you're going to frighten me.' Tim's voice had a nervous edge to it.

'Oh don't be such a baby. Hurry up with that bag.' Chris was already half-way into the attic, the candle casting an enormous shadow of his head and shoulders around the cramped space. Tim crept in on all fours afraid of banging his head on the rafters, imagining the spiders waiting for him in every nook and cranny. In the light of the candle he could see three shelves of green cooking apples.

'Ruddy mice have been at them,' said Chris, 'and some have gone rotten. They must have been touching each other.' He put a dozen or so into the bag. 'That's it, let's go.'

Soon after they got back downstairs Marie O'Brien, a dark-haired slim girl dressed completely in black, pushed her pram round the corner of the house. 'Can you help me up the steps with it?'

'Please?' Chris mouthed the word silently towards Tim, who started giggling. They heaved the ancient pram into the kitchen, where it occupied much of the spare floor space. Marie took off her coat and scarf and put the baby in a small baby-chair on the kitchen table. Annie climbed up to stroke the baby's face. It smiled, and a globule of milky sick ran down onto its bib. Annie quickly drew back.

'Can you fetch me some milk for his bottle, and get the tin of rusks out, will you?' Already the requests were starting to keep the boys busy as Marie set about commandeering their precious food rations. The boys grudgingly obliged, but pulled rude faces behind her back. Chris thought she was much too young to have a baby, and where was the father?

They went out into the garden, bored. Then, turning their bikes upside down, they pushed bits of cardboard into the spokes. As they pedalled like mad with their hands, a trumpeting sound ensued, rising and falling with the vigour of their pedalling.

'Stop making that awful noise,' demanded Marie. 'It's upsetting the baby.' They wandered off up the garden idly hitting at thistles with sticks.

The first signs of spring were already visible. Snowdrops and crocuses were still in bloom, though nearly over, while the swelling heads of daffodils still needed a spell of warm sunshine to coax them open. Hazel bushes cascaded with lambs' tails, which shook tremulously in the late winter wind.

'Come in for tea,' called Marie. She had cut thick slices of bread from a new loaf, ignoring the half-finished piece on the bread board, and had wiped them with butter and blackcurrant jam, from a newly opened but already half empty pot. Purple stains around Marie's mouth and the baby's indicated where the rest had gone. Tim and Chris exchanged glances at this flagrant extravagance.

'We always have the first piece plain,' accused Tim. 'Nonsense,' replied Marie, walking round the kitchen with a thick sandwich oozing jam at its edges. 'Mmmm . . . lovely!'

With tea over and cleared away, Marie asked, 'What's behind that door on the landing?' She had clearly been snooping while the boys were outside. Chris was non-committal, some intuitive feeling warning him to be cautious, but she persisted. 'Would you take me up and show me?'

Chris led the way through the attic door, shielding a candle with his hand. Marie stooped and followed in behind him. 'Ooh, what lovely apples,' she said, prodding at them with her fingers. 'The same as the ones downstairs. I'm sure your mother wouldn't mind if I took a few home for myself.' She was already scooping the biggest and best into her apron, which acted as a makeshift bag.

Chris thought for a split second, then made up his mind. Pushing past Marie, he dived out of the attic, extinguishing the candle as he went, and locked the door behind him. A pitiful shriek came from inside, followed by banging on the door. The screaming that followed slowly subsided

4. *Marie steals apples in the attic*

into sobbing and pleading. The boys looked at each other with a sense of achievement, but with some apprehension. What had they done?

Their mother heard the rumpus as she got off the bus at the top of the road and quickened her pace. Chris hid in the sitting room while Tim did his best to explain what had happened. Little Annie was shocked into wide-eyed silence.

With Marie released, and placated with a bag of apples and a pot of homemade jam, his mother tried to explain to Chris what a terrible thing he had done; that this sort of thing must NEVER happen again, however much in the wrong the other person had been. Chris defended himself and his actions vigorously, and thought he could detect a certain support from his mother. He risked a quick sidelong glance at her, and was forgiven with a hug and a cuddle. She added decisively, 'I don't think we'll be having Marie and her baby back to this house again, will we?'

6
NEW NEIGHBOURS AND A BIRTHDAY PARTY

It was a misty September morning just before the start of the new school term. Tim dragged himself out of bed. There was a distinct autumnal chill in the air. A few days earlier the cat had produced four kittens, and that night, carrying them gently one by one in her mouth from under the wardrobe where she had given birth, she had brought them into his bed. Now they were all tucked up under the eiderdown near the foot of the bed. Tim listened to their constant mewing and felt their little bodies wriggling close to his feet.

Sitting on the third stair down, he peered through the knot-hole into the kitchen and watched Mother scraping lard from an old cracked pudding basin into the frying pan. The sound of sizzling and the irresistible smell of frying bacon soon wafted up the stairs.

'Call Chris down, will you? He must have his hair cut today ready for school.'

The boys sat down at the table and picked up their mugs of tea. Annie wandered round the kitchen aimlessly, clearly not hungry.

'Who's got the ticking mug?' asked Chris. There was a silence as they all listened.

'I think it's me,' announced Tim proudly, his mug pressed against his ear. His mother smiled.

One of the four white straight-sided mugs had a flaw in its glazing, which allowed liquid to seep into the fabric of the pottery, thereby setting up tension. After a few minutes a repetitive clicking noise was given out. It was a cause for some pride to be the temporary owner of the ticking mug.

'Why doesn't my mug tick?' asked Annie, waving her plastic Peter Rabbit mug at her mother and asking for more orangeade.

'Never mind, dear. You'll soon be old enough to drink out of the white mugs like the boys. Now I'm afraid we're out of marmalade till I've made some more, so you'll have to make do with plain for today. Oh and Chris, we need some potatoes and a cabbage for lunch. Could you be a dear and get some from the garden, please?'

'How can I when you've told me to get my hair cut?' he replied angrily, jumping up from the table and getting his bike out of the shed.

Tim grudgingly agreed to help and was given a large plastic bowl and a sharp knife. As he passed the open door of the larder he looked in at the wasp trap. A jam-jar full of sugary water caught these ever-present pests as they pushed their way through a tear in the perforated zinc that covered the window frame. Tim was morbidly fascinated by the death struggles of the drowning wasps as they paddled round inside the jar, unable to struggle out.

He wandered up the garden path alongside the privet hedge, where, as a much younger child, he had 'kept his imaginary pigs'. Every morning they had to be fed with a watery gruel of earth and grass, ladled out from a bucket into the hollows under the hedge. His mother smiled and watched this daily ritual from the kitchen door, sometimes even inviting neighbours to join her. Once it had become established as a party-piece Tim had become self-conscious and no longer did it.

As Tim passed the artichoke bed he tried to put out of his mind those tasteless globes of white, pithy mush that his mother sometimes tried to pass off as potatoes, and came to the vegetable garden proper. Here, rows of neatly planted cabbages, sprouts, onions, cauliflowers and leeks were home to dozens of white butterflies and green caterpillars. Here, as in countless other gardens in Britain, vegetables and fruit provided the mainstay of the family's food supply. The lessons of the First World War, when malnutrition and even starvation were a problem in many large cities, had been well learnt by the authorities. Frequent wireless broadcasts and newspaper articles helped to persuade families to 'grow their own'.

Tim uprooted a dozen or so potatoes and cut a cabbage. His chore completed, he continued to the orchard feeling comfortably relaxed.

In the branches of a small fir tree, which was oozing sticky globules of resin from its bark, Tim spotted a family of long-tailed tits, and what he thought was a mouse working its way in jerky movements up a damson tree turned out to be a tree-creeper. Higher up, a squirrel was swinging untidily from branch to branch, before dropping onto the half-collapsed wooden fence behind to reach the nut bushes. These seemed to be for ever growing out of control and causing territorial disputes with the neighbours. But at least the squirrels enjoyed the nuts, which never seemed to be ripe at Christmas when the boys wanted them.

Tim's reverie continued uninterrupted for a while, until a voice broke into his peaceful thoughts. 'Can I play?' It was Brian Priddy, poking his head round the corner of the house. 'I've just met Chris on his bike and he said it was OK.'

'Well, don't let Mum see. You know she thinks you're a nuisance.'

With Brian around things immediately brightened up. They peered into the corrugated-iron pig-pen to see what Willie was up to. Many families kept a pig during wartime. It was an essential part of the meat ration and was fed on peelings from the kitchen, leftovers, and food that had gone off, mixed into a gruel with pig-nuts. When it was fat it was collected, slaughtered and taken to the local butcher who kept the carcase in his cold-store to be cut into joints, chops, ham and bacon. Very little went to waste; the children ate chitterlings, liver, kidneys and tongue, all the by-products of this noble and friendly beast. The day that the slaughtermen came to collect the pig was a day of achievement. But after the first occasion, when the weeping children had watched it being chased round the garden by men with sticks, terrified and squealing loudly as it was driven into the waiting lorry, their mother always made sure that they were sent away to a neighbour's house.

Tim hit the side of the pen with a stick, which shook and heaved as the pig roused himself from his morning doze, hoping that the interruption meant food. Brian gobbed at him, hitting him on the head, before finding a small frog in the grass which he tossed into the pig's trough. Willie snapped at it several times before managing to scoff it down. Egged on by this piece of daring, Brian shinned up into the spindly plum tree that overhung the pen, and shook it like mad. By now many of the plums were over-ripe and splashed onto the pig's back, surrounding him in a cloud of sleepy wasps. He gobbled up the plums greedily, stones and all, but flicked his ears angrily at the wasps and was not best pleased when they stung him.

Brian, getting over-excited, ripped open his flies and directed a well-aimed stream of wee over the pig's head and back. Tim flinched at this disgusting behaviour, but Willie appeared to enjoy it as it soothed the wasp stings.

'I hope you're all behaving yourselves,' came a call from the kitchen, as Chris appeared shaking his head and rubbing his neck to remove the stray hairs left there by the barber.

'Yes, Mum, just talking to Willie,' shouted Tim, as Brian, hearing their mother's voice, decided it was time to leave.

Having lost interest in Willie, Chris and Tim made for the largest apple tree in the far corner of the orchard and started climbing – carefully avoiding the axle grease that had been wiped round the top of the trunk to trap insects before they could reach the blossom and buds and do damage. Tim peered with pity and distaste at the entombed bodies of ants, earwigs, woodlice and flies caught in this sticky orange goo. A swing of the leg and a violent twist of the body and Chris was up on the lowest branch, with Tim just behind. Then, thrusting steadily upwards, they reached the top, their bare legs scratched, ankles bruised, shins grazed, and faces hit by ripe apples. Once out in the bright sunlight amongst the rasping of hover-flies and humming of bees, and his face refreshed by a gentle breeze, Tim was able to experience that feeling of exhilaration and peace that he valued so much.

He cast an eye over the garden. Next to the house the buddleia shrubs were still attracting butterflies, and the elderberry bushes were now being attacked by birds for their fruit. Soon window ledges, car windscreens and worst of all white shirts on the washing line would be spattered with their purple droppings. Mother cat had stretched herself out in the cat-mint and was being pestered by her kittens. A nearby wren ticked angrily at them; a blackbird sang lustily from a chimney-pot; and a robin in a tall ash tree filled the air with its watery song, a harbinger of the winter to come.

Tim looked round at other familiar landmarks. Far over the valley the chalk downs rose towards the skyline. Tim wondered afresh, as he always did, who lived in that white-painted mansion that stood silhouetted against a wood. Was it the squire, with servants and gardeners, or was it perhaps a school or a nursing home? Much closer, behind him, were the neatly kept gardens of the terraced houses, which stretched along the main road higher up.

Mother had finished hanging out the washing and was collecting gooseberries in a colander for lunch. Chris spotted her, and clutched his hands to his stomach in a theatrical gesture, 'Oh no! Not goosegogs again. I hope there's tons of sugar to put on them!' Tim laughed. He felt much the same about stewed gooseberries.

To their utter amazement they suddenly heard other boys' voices just a few yards away. The top of an apple tree in the next-door garden threshed about wildly and, to the sound of snapping twigs and muffled curses, two dishevelled heads emerged. For a time nothing was said as the four boys eyed each other up with furtive sidelong looks. Eventually Chris broke the ice. 'What are you doing there?'

'We live here.'

'You can't do, the house is empty.'

'Well we do because we moved in yesterday.'

Silence fell.

'Is yours a big house?'

'Yes, it's got two bedrooms upstairs.'

'Sounds small to me, ours has got four.'

This gave Chris and Tim something to think about, since the previous owner of the next-door house had been a little old lady who owned lots of cats. They had never been inside. They wondered if the new neighbours would become friends or whether the mutual suspicion would continue.

Tim did not know what to think, but cheered up at the thought of some new friends close by.

A call came from the next-door house. 'Come on in, you two. It's dinner-time. Come and wash your hands.'

'Well, we've got to go in now,' said the elder of the two boys, 'Maybe see you again soon.'

5. The Mason boys meet the Keelings

Tim scrambled down from the apple tree to tell his mother of the great new discovery. Chris followed more thoughtfully, answering little Annie's questions as they walked down the path.

'I met Mrs Keeling earlier this morning and we had a good chat,' said Mrs Mason as she prepared their midday meal. 'They seem a nice family, and believe it or not they also have a little girl, a bit older than Annie. Their father's in the Forces too: he's a major in the Medical Corps.'

'Well, I thought the older boy's a bit of a drip,' said Chris, trying to sound superior.

'And so's his younger brother,' added Tim, not to be outdone.

'Nonsense, dear, you hardly know them. I'm sure you'll all be the best of friends in no time.' Chris was not so sure, and pulled a rude face.

It was the afternoon of Helen Borrodaile's birthday party. Accompanied by groans and complaints, the boys were made to wash thoroughly and put on clean shirts and best trousers. 'Find me your shoes and I'll polish them,' said Mother, determined to have the boys looking as smart as possible in spite of their patched and hand-me-down clothes. 'I've bought her a nice Famous Five book as a present; all girls like Enid Blyton. Now off you go and make sure you thank her afterwards. Be good!'

The party, with its mix of children of varying ages, was perhaps inevitably a trying affair for all concerned. Mr Borrodaile, a quiet man and not a natural party host, tried to organise rounders in the garden, while his wife played games with the girls indoors. After a short time chaos broke out on the lawn as the boys rolled about on the grass letting off steam. From through the window various pairs of eyes watched enviously as the girls cast glances at the boys of their choice. Finally a weary Mr Borrodaile called everyone in for tea.

'Well done, dear, you've certainly worn them out,' commented his mild and ever-helpful wife from the kitchen, as she passed plates of sandwiches and jam-filled scones through the serving hatch. A scrum developed round the dining room table as the boys squabbled for seats. The girls looked on with pained expressions as they joined them.

'Will you have orange or lemon squash?' asked Mrs Borrodaile.

'Both!' spluttered Brian Priddy, guffawing with laughter and showering the table with crumbs. Some children giggled.

The birthday cake was finally brought in, a sponge with three coloured layers, and coated in icing-sugar. Little silver balls spelled out Helen's name on the top. She simpered self-consciously as the nine candles were lit, slowly leaning over the table to relish her moment of glory. Brian Priddy timed his move to perfection. With a scattering of plates he lurched forward, extinguishing the first four candles with a blast of his breath. Helen burst into tears, and only regained her composure when all nine had been relit. Mrs Borrodaile, always so mild-mannered, said in a strained voice, 'Brian, that wasn't a very kind thing to do. I think you'd better eat your piece of birthday cake in the kitchen.'

Once the tea things had been cleared away it was time for more games, which proceeded with varying levels of success. Pass the parcel was stopped after three boys fought over the package and reduced it to shreds. Musical chairs had to end when two of the fatter boys threw themselves onto a rather frail chair and broke its leg.

A quieter game was suggested, at which the boys groaned and some of the girls looked relieved. Michael Borrodaile was sent out of the room and blindfolded. His father gave instructions. 'Wait by the door. That's right. Now three paces forward. One pace to the left, and another, Not too fast. Now . . . stop!' But too late. The children laughed and clapped as he bumped against an armchair. Two others had a go, including Tim. One girl managed to complete the obstacle course without bumping into any of the furniture by listening very carefully to the instructions. In a moment of inspiration Mr Borrodaile asked Brian to be the last participant. 'But be very careful.

While you're being blindfolded we're going to rearrange the furniture so there's no use trusting to memory. OK?' He was taken into the kitchen and the blindfold put on. Many minutes passed as he listened to the scraping of chairs and muffled giggles from the girls.

Back in the sitting room he followed his instructions to a tee, managing to steer clear of the bulkier bits of furniture. Several times he touched the walls but was guided back into the centre of the room. Initially full of bravado, he thought he was doing terribly well, but slowly doubts entered his mind. As he moved towards some quietly sniggering girl he leant down to touch the chair she was sitting on. He could feel nothing. More sniggers and the sound of muffled feet made him suspicious, in spite of Mr Borrodaile's continuing instructions. But as he fumbled along the curtains by the bay window he finally smelt a rat and tore off his blindfold. Not only was the room cleared of all the smaller pieces of furniture, but the armchairs were piled on the sofa. What's more, the other children had mysteriously vanished; only Mr Borrodaile remained.

'That'll teach you,' said Chris, as the others returned to the sitting room laughing and clapping their hands with glee. Unusually for him, Brian was lost for words. Pressing a handkerchief to his eyes, he fled the room and ran out of the house.

7
UNCLE JOHN'S FARM

'Bill will be here soon. It's Saturday,' said Mrs Mason, knowing it would drag the boys from their beds. Bill Hardiman was the driver of the Bedford lorry which called at the house most weekends from their uncle's farm twelve miles away. For the struggling fatherless family this was a glorious haven of plentiful food, where the dogs barked joyously, the cook laughed and the sun always seemed to shine.

They all liked Bill – Chris because on trips to the farm Bill let him steer the lorry when the road was safe; Tim because he could sit in the driver's seat when the lorry was parked outside the house, twisting and turning the steering wheel pretending to drive it; and their mother because he brought them eggs and the occasional chicken or joint of meat from her much-loved brother.

Sitting in the cab Tim savoured the smell of old oily leather and noted the corn sacks that covered the splits in the seats where the stuffing burst through. Spanners, a jack, rags and rope lay in the passenger footwell and in the back were more tools and sacks, a tarpaulin, fruit boxes and empty milk churns. Blue smoke puffed up through gaps in the floor when the engine was running.

'And we're all invited to Sunday lunch tomorrow, so that'll be a treat for us all.'

'Yippee', 'Great', 'Terrific', 'Marvellous': the boys expressed their delight with whoops of joy. 'Hope it's roast chicken again. Yummy!'

'Can we go up on the downs?'

'And visit the ponds and do some fishing?'

'Boring! Let's look for birds' eggs, or better still hunt for rifle bullets at the ranges.' Their ideas came thick and fast.

'I suppose those dreadful cousins will be there,' added Chris, putting a dampener on their enthusiasm.

'Don't be so rude and ungrateful,' scolded Mother. You must learn to get on with your cousins. They're polite and well-mannered girls. You'd better wear your old clothes knowing what you'll be up to, but make sure they're clean.'

Sunday promised to be a warm late autumn day. The family caught the bus into town, an open-topped double-decker with slatted wooden seats, which cut into their legs, and a curving staircase outside. Chris and Tim rushed to the front to 'steer' the bus through the town while their mother sat further back away from the draught, cuddling Annie.

At the bus station they transferred to a single-decker and again the front seats were free. Annie was upset by the bluebottles struggling to escape from the window. 'Don't be such a baby,' scoffed Tim as he rushed to the front of the bus. He loved to look along its bonnet and out over the headlight that wobbled on the mudguard. The other passengers, all dressed in their Sunday best, were carrying cakes, homemade jam and knitted garments to pass on to their relatives in the country.

At last the regimental badges cut by soldiers during the First World War appeared on the chalk hillsides, and they got off the bus. The air here felt quite different. A warm breeze soughed gently in the clump of fir trees at the top of the gravel track that led down to the farm, their resinous scent adding to the children's rising feeling of anticipation. Chaffinches sang in the taller of the hawthorn bushes on either side and plovers stood one-legged in the fields, facing into the breeze.

They were greeted by a terrific leaping and barking from the dogs penned up in a wire cage outside the back door. 'Poor doggies,' said Annie, sympathetically.

'They're not pets,' replied Tim, showing off the knowledge he had acquired from Chris on his last visit. 'They're working dogs, trained to pick up pheasants and partridges on shoots. They're not allowed to get too friendly with people or they won't do their job properly.'

'Come and hang your coats up. How are you all? Did you have a good journey? Have you boys been behaving yourselves? And how's little Annie – though not so little any more?' She stroked Annie's cheek, who twisted her face away and hid behind her mother's leg. 'Oh dear, still shy are we?' Aunt Elizabeth led them into the house as the women chatted and laughed. This was a day for good company and relaxation. Already marvellous smells were coming from the kitchen.

'Morning, Mrs Mason, and how are we all today?'

'Oh, pretty well, thanks, Cookie. And you? Keeping busy?'

'I'll say so. Master had a shoot yesterday and then there were sixteen for supper last night. So you can see they keep me on my toes!'

'I'll bet they do. Cookie, you're a real treasure!' The boys hovered at the door until the friendly cook waved them in, giving each a hug. Chris looked expectantly at the larder.

'You really are a pair of monkeys. Well let's see. There may be a bit of yesterday's treacle tart left over somewhere. Yes, here it is, tucked away in the corner. Now make sure it doesn't spoil your dinner.' She cut two generous pieces and watched with pleasure as they were eaten. Cookie always made a drama of this ritual. She knew that boys were always hungry – and especially the Mason boys.

As they went to the sitting room to join the others they heard giggles from upstairs on the landing. Angela and Trudy, their two cousins, peered over the banisters whispering between themselves, but did not come down. Aunt Elizabeth was explaining to her sister-in-law that John was still out on the farm and that the boys could go off for an hour or so. 'Lunch is at one sharp, so don't be late.' What a marvellous feeling of release as they left the grown-ups and shot outside into the sunlight past the barking dogs.

Facing the house was a large stone building, originally a stable block but now with its central courtyard floored over to provide much extra space. Finding one's way around this labyrinth was difficult but Chris knew it well, so, passing a threshing machine, a binder and two David Brown tractors, he made straight for a door in the rear wall. The unexpected gloom as they climbed the dusty and cobweb-filled stairs behind confused Tim. And while the acrid smell that drifted downwards stung his nostrils and almost overpowered him, it was above all the pervasive sound of countless tiny chirping voices that mesmerised him. The sight – and the smell – that met him at the top of the stairs took his breath away, for the upper storey of the barn was home to thousands of chickens, separated by age and size into a series of pens. The tiniest chicks, mere balls of yellow fluff, were looked after by broody hens held behind bars in wooden coops. In each pen there were water troughs and feed trays with electric lamps overhead, keeping them warm in the artificially lengthened day that speeded up their growth. The pungent stench of ammonia and the claustrophobic atmosphere almost overwhelmed Tim as Chris said, 'Let's get out and look at the tractors. I could do with some fresh air!'

'Mary, is there anything your children won't eat? Stuffing, bread sauce, chipolatas? A bit of everything, then?' Uncle John stood at the head of the table about to carve the roast chicken. The boys nodded vigorously.

'Yes thanks, John,' replied his sister, 'but only a small helping for Annie.' They all tucked in as Cookie went to fetch more gravy. 'Have you heard from James or Pat lately?' she continued. These were their other two brothers, both in the army and serving overseas. John, being a farmer, was in a reserved occupation and not allowed to join up, though he often wished he could.

'Yes. We had a letter from Pat in North Africa only a week ago. Things seem to be a bit grim there, with Rommel pushing everyone back towards Alexandria. They seem determined to capture the Suez Canal.' The family ate in silence for a moment.

'Isn't there talk of that new chap Montgomery replacing the Auk?' Mother asked.

Tim suppressed a snigger. 'I thought that was a bird!' he half-whispered.

Chris scoffed. 'They're talking about General Auchinlech, silly.'

Serious discussion about the progress of the war continued between the adults, while the boys cast sidelong glances towards their cousins – too shy to speak to them directly.

Auntie Beth led the conversation on to a brighter topic. 'Jim's going to be a father again. Muriel's expecting some time in November. He's still at Aldershot on secondment after Dunkirk. He's probably too old to be sent abroad again, thank God. They came down for a few days in the summer and Muriel judged at the Flower Show. She was about to award me second prize for my dahlias but was pointed towards Mrs Grove's nasturtiums at the last minute. There's always a terrible fuss if the vicar's wife doesn't win something every year!'

John laughed. 'And Jim joined the farm team against the village and scored twenty-three not out. Nearly carried the day. We had to deck him out in some of my old whites – much too tight, of course. He damn near split the crotch cow-shotting a six into the barley-field.'

'Please don't use that word at the table.' Aunt Beth cast a reproving look at her husband.

'"Damn" is not swearing – just a good old English expletive,' replied her husband, irritated. He was starting to get tetchy; the strain of running a large farm with inadequate labour under wartime restrictions was beginning to tell.

It was perhaps not a good moment for his sister to ask, 'Was it a good harvest this year, John?'

'No. Bloody awful. Yields were down and the grain needed a lot of drying.' Aunt Beth rolled her eyes towards the ceiling in despair as he continued, pretending not to notice her anger. 'There was too much rain in June, which encouraged mould, and with most of the youngsters away in the army or earning a packet doing factory work for the war effort there was no one to pull up the wild oats.'

Aunt Beth crossed to the serving hatch to call the maid. 'Don't let's talk about the farm and its problems, dear, you know it just gets you upset. And after all, it *is* Sunday.'

Uncle John sulked as the maid collected the dishes. The girls had only picked at their food and Chris was aghast at the waste: it would never be allowed at home. Tim had carefully saved the best bits of chicken till last, and as he turned to his aunt to answer a question about school the maid briskly gathered his plate onto the pile with the others. 'But I . . . please, I . . .' His mother, spotting the drama unfolding, laughingly asked for the plate to be put back. Tim flushed with embarrassment as all eyes were directed towards him.

After a delicious chocolate sponge-pudding the youngsters were allowed to leave the table while the adults went into the sitting-room for coffee. Uncle John took a silver cigarette case from his pocket and, turning in the doorway, said, 'Now just be careful, you boys. They're bale-carting in the seven acre field by the road, so don't get in the way or you might get hurt. And make sure you're back in plenty of time for tea.'

With the constraints of being sociable at the meal table over, the boys rushed outside again. The girls stayed in the sitting room with their parents and played at being nurses to little Annie. With the sun warm on their faces and the dusty chalk of the trackways catching in their throats, Chris and Tim were attracted towards the sound of revving engines. Over the hedge they could see the top of a rick. Bales spewed off the top of an elevator and were pushed into position by Alby Blake while his younger brother Joshua heaved them on at the bottom with a prong. At the far end of the field two ancient open-topped saloon cars with long wooden rakes on the front were scooping up the bales and bringing them over to the elevator.

Bill Hardiman shouted from an old Austin 10, 'Come on over. Climb aboard. But hold on tight, this will be pretty bumpy.'

The car had no doors and the shiny leather seat was covered in dust and straw. Bill smiled as two pairs of white-knuckled hands gripped the dashboard. With a crashing and grinding of gears it jerked and bumped its way across the field, its steering wheel juddering almost uncontrollably over the furrows and stubble. Bales were swept up until the rakes could hold no more, then were deposited at the elevator as the car set out for a further load. Suddenly, with an almighty crash, the windscreen flopped onto the bonnet in a shower of broken glass. The boys looked nervous as Bill laughed, 'Had enough for today, have we?'

'I think it's about time we went back for tea,' said Chris, much to Tim's relief. 'Will we see you next Saturday as usual?'

Bill nodded and, waving cheerfully, swung the car around.

✳ ✳ ✳

With the day drawing to a close, their mother suggested a slow ramble onto the downs behind the farm to settle their tea. For her this was the culmination of a perfect day, a return to the private place she had escaped to as a troubled teenager all those years earlier. Her brother knew how important this was to her and said willingly, 'We'll look after Annie. She'll be no trouble for a couple of hours, and the girls adore her.'

Their route led them past farm sheds, behind the dairy and towards the foot of the downs. The chalky path soon skirted a group of derelict brick buildings, a relic of the firing ranges built in the First World War to train the riflemen of Kitchener's New Army. Chris dashed behind an old store room where he had spotted some empty rifle cartridges, and emerged stuffing them into his pockets. Tim and his mother pressed on up the rapidly steepening path, their feet occasionally dislodging lumps of chalk that trickled back down towards the farm. Chris caught up with them, and together they stood overlooking the badges, those chalk-cut symbols frozen in time of the regiments that had spent so many weeks of their war duty perfecting the accuracy of their rifle fire. Tim marvelled at their enormous size, cut as if by giants from the downland turf, unable to imagine how such intricate designs could have been transferred onto the blank canvas of a grassy hillside. From their vantage point he gazed around into the hazy distance of blue shimmering hills, of grey-green woods, of ochre-coloured fields awaiting the plough. In the valley below his eye followed the snaking line of the river as it passed from farm to farm and from village to village. He sat down next to his mother on the springy turf nibbled short by sheep, and tried to avoid the thistles that pricked at the back of his bare legs.

Chaffinches sang in the thorn, hornbeam and yew bushes, the last remnant of the hillside's ancient flora. In the ash, elderberry and nut bushes alongside the drovers' road, which stretched the length of this backbone of chalk downland, yellowhammers repeated their 'little bit of bread and *no* cheese' song. Larks rose and fell joyously in the scented air around them. Mrs Mason felt her spirit renewing itself amongst the familiar yellow cowslips, blue scabious and delicate bee orchids, and a deep feeling of peace and fulfilment overwhelmed her.

A yell from Chris roused his dozing mother. She sat up quickly, shading her eyes from the low angle of the sun. 'Look, over there! He's

6. *A German fighter over Uncle's farm*

coming this way!' All three were now on their feet as the rasping throb of an aero engine sputtered and roared a short distance away. High in the sky two Hurricane fighters were slipping through the late afternoon air towards them, chasing their unseen quarry at high speed.

'Look! It's a Jerry fighter!' shouted Chris. 'An Me 109 . . . it's in trouble . . . behind those trees!' With an ear-splitting roar the pale blue underside of the fighter crossed in front of them, only feet above the ground and pouring clouds of black smoke from its engine. The pilot had already opened his canopy and was struggling with the controls, desperate to drag some last vestige of life from the stricken engine before it finally fell silent.

'He's too low to bale out . . . he'll kill himself.' Chris was beside himself with excitement, caught up in the drama of the moment. The Hurricanes swept over them as the German fighter made one last bid for height as it headed out over the valley. It rolled onto its back, releasing a bundle that tumbled twice before transforming itself into a parachute. The plane plummeted into a wood and exploded, the pilot drifting through the rising cloud of smoke, circled by the watching British fighters. They rocked their wings to him, in recognition of a fellow aviator who had flown his last wartime mission and now only faced a long period of captivity. The boys' mother put her arms round Tim's shoulders and said resignedly, 'Even here you can't get away from this wretched war.'

8
A BROKEN LEG AND ANNIE GOES MISSING

The war was now in its third year and seemed to drag on relentlessly. Provisions from the 'Top Shop', Mr Woodhead's little general stores at the top of the road, were mostly rationed and often ran out. There were frequent shortages of sugar, jam, butter and meat. Unnecessary luxury items were not available at all; tropical fruit and chocolate were unheard of. While freighters were being sunk in steadily increasing numbers by U-boats in the North Atlantic, it was almost exclusively war materials that were being risked in the convoys now.

Chris in particular had vivid memories of the pre-war days, even his early childhood in India, of travel in England without restrictions, of the family car. Tim, being younger, barely remembered these days at all; he was much more conscious of the present atmosphere, mostly brought about by the lack of fathers in his friends' houses and of the seemingly never-ending conversations between adults about 'this damn war' with its 'wretched shortages' and the 'real hardships' they were all suffering.

But today was a still warm autumn Saturday. The trees were in their rich October colours, though, after a mid-week of storms and rain, they had just started to lose their leaves. Tim rushed down the back steps onto the lawn, breathing in the fresh air deeply and glad to be out of the stuffy house. He inadvertently frightened a cock pheasant and three hen-birds that had been feeding there. They flew up, startled, and rocketed over the hedge.

'Look after Annie for a bit will you, dear?' his mother called from the back door. 'She wants to play outside but I really must get on with this pile of ironing.'

'Oh, all right, if I must. But she spoils everything,' groaned Tim.

Chris joined him, calling out cheerfully, 'Just leave her alone. She's OK. Now, you stand between those bushes. That's the goal. When I've scored ten we'll change over. Right?' He seemed to be in an excellent mood. Annie tried to join in, but found it too rough so she went into the shed to get out her latest birthday present – a superb red pedal car, bought secondhand from a better-off friend of the family.

The impromptu football practice continued, but was dominated by Chris who was too fast for Tim. Then there was a cautious whistle from near the corner of the house. An unruly mop of ginger hair appeared briefly but was quickly withdrawn. 'Psst! Come here.' It was Brian Priddy, trying as usual to avoid the boys' mother. 'Let's go down to those bombed-out houses by the gasworks. James Hammond says there's lots to find there.'

Tim felt, and looked, extremely doubtful. He thought of the long bike ride to get there, well beyond where his mother normally let him go. But Chris had no such reservations. 'Annie!' he shouted. 'Mum wants you indoors. Go inside now.' Annie rubbed her eyes and pretended to cry. She hated the way the boys pushed her around, and were able to go off whenever they wanted to. She sat in her little car and watched them enviously as they disappeared on their bikes.

The boys sped down the road, collecting an older boy, Robert Higgins, as they went. They passed Moore's garage and cycled under the old medieval wall of the cathedral, where Robert pointed out the gargoyles and Norman dog-tooth decorations in the stonework, once part of an earlier abbey. Freewheeling through one archway and out through another, they passed along a Georgian terrace near the railway station. Once close to the gasworks they entered an area of mean narrow streets and ugly terraced houses alongside the railway lines, where bombs had fallen. One house had been almost demolished, several badly damaged, and windows in the entire street had been boarded up. Clearly a German bomber, either lost during a raid on a more distant city or following the railway lines on a moonlit night, had decided to jettison his bombs onto this 'target of opportunity'.

Pushing their bikes into a narrow alley, the four boys scouted around until they found some movable slats in the rear fence of one of the bombed buildings. The three eldest slipped through.

'Keep *cave*, Tim. Give a whistle if anyone comes, and guard the bikes.'

'What about me? Aren't I allowed to come in too?' Tim fought back his disappointment.

'You can have a look round later. Come on, you two!' Brian was in his element, taking charge and egging on others in yet another of his nefarious and dubious ventures.

Tim peered through the fence. Inside he could see piles of blackened rubble, stark jagged walls, exposed and tilted floors. The site had been hurriedly fenced off, but because of a shortage of manpower, not very securely. Already golden-rod, purple loose-strife and buddleia were growing out of the rich soil of what were once carefully tended gardens. Butterflies danced around the sweet-smelling shrubs extracting nectar.

Tim squatted down, leaning against the fence already warmed by the sun. He was apprehensive. What if someone came? What should he say? The bikes clearly showed that there were other boys around. He listened to the muffled sound of loose bricks falling, of wooden floorboards shifting and excited cries of discovery from inside the damaged building. The voices receded, the scrabbling died away and suddenly there was a boastful shout from high up on a dividing wall. Brian was silhouetted against an exposed first-floor fireplace, with Chris balancing on a collapsed floor lower down. Robert was nowhere to be seen.

'Don't make such a row, you blithering halfwit,' Chris called up at Brian, his hands cupped to his mouth in a hoarse stage shout. 'You'll attract half the street.' Brian responded by working his way round a dangerously unstable chimney-stack and dropping out of sight.

Tim pushed his way through the fence to get a better view, still overawed by the devastation around him. Idly he picked up a loose brick, bright orange on one side but acrid-smelling and black on the other. He marvelled at the sign of new life in the shrubs and butterflies that had colonised this site of dereliction. The sound of footsteps and an occasional muffled curse told him that the others were returning, feeling that they had pushed their luck far enough.

'Everything OK?' Chris asked. 'Take a look at this.' In his hand he held a sizeable and thick fragment of jagged metal, already well rusted. 'It's part of a German bomb casing. Careful, the edges are sharp.'

Tim took it from him and peered closely, amazed at its heavy weight. 'I can't see any German writing on it. Are you sure it's real?'

Chris groaned at his naïveté. Turning to see what Robert had found, the boys were amused to see him holding a chipped brown teapot and a teddy bear with a leg missing. They all laughed.

Engrossed in their finds, they failed to hear the heavy but quiet footfall behind the fence – but suddenly noticed a blue helmet moving about near their parked bikes. Tim made a dash for the fence just as a dark blue arm pushed through the gap and grasped the lapel of his jerkin. A red face and bushy moustache followed the arm. 'And what, may I ask, are you up to?' The constable sounded kindly but firm. Their noisy activity had alerted a passer-by, who had rung the police. 'And you two had better come out as well, so we can all have a little chat. I'm not sure my old bones, let alone my stomach, can squeeze through this gap in the fence.'

Brushing the soot and brick dust off their clothes, they all stood sheepishly in front of the policeman.

'I imagine you all go to school and have learnt to read,' he continued. 'There are notices all over the place saying 'DANGER – KEEP OUT'. They are there as a warning, to prevent nasty accidents happening to young men like you.'

'We didn't see any,' mumbled Chris in an unconvincing manner.

'Funny, there's one right next to your bikes: look! Right then, we'd better have some names and addresses. Let's start with you, sonny.' The constable pulled out his notebook and pencil and looked towards Robert.

'Er . . . John Smith, 22 Coronation Rise.' He looked up hopefully and was greeted by a stony stare.

'Would that be the Coronation Rise on the street sign over there? How very convenient. Now, let's start again, shall we? And please, no more John Smiths, my book's full of them.'

Grudgingly the three gave their names and addresses, and waited nervously as Chris asked what would happen next.

'Oh that's very simple. First it's down to the station, then three or four nights in the cells. Mind you, the grub's pretty poor – just bread and water. Then up before the beak on Friday morning, and sentencing. Five years minimum I should think, maybe transportation or a visit to the Tower of London. And you know what that means.' He ran his finger across the front of his throat, winking.

Tim was struggling to come to terms with this play-acting: was any of it true? The older boys managed a wan smile and began to cheer up a little.

'Now I'll tell you what I'm really going to do. Each of your parents will be informed and asked to keep a closer eye on you in future. We know who you are now, so if there's any more bother you'll be for the high jump. OK? Now get off home, straight away.'

'My father's going to kill me,' said Robert with feeling.

'That's the whole idea,' smiled the constable, putting away his notebook and pencil.

'Everything all right, Bill?' came a shout from the end of the alley. 'Dealt with the little blighters, have you?'

'Yes, fine thanks, Sarge. But there's a spare bike here so there's another one still to nab.'

As if on cue there came the sound of falling brickwork, followed by Brian's angry shouting. 'What's going on? Have you three pushed off and left me to it? Come and see what I've found. There's a kitchen cabinet full of stuff here just waiting to be nicked.'

'Oh is there?' shouted the sergeant, pushing his way through the gap in the fence. 'Well, my advice to you is to stay exactly where you are and not move an inch.'

Brian, realising he was in real trouble, pulled himself free from the floor joists he was hanging on to and tried to climb higher away from the policeman. Loose bricks showered down in all directions as the sergeant tried to cut him off. Determined to find a way back to his bike for a quick getaway, Brian scaled a partition wall, put his weight on a projecting floorboard, which gave way, and lurched against a chimney-breast.

'Stop, you little idiot! Don't touch that. Come down now while you're still in one piece.' The sergeant was getting angry and anxious, and his concern was conveyed to the constable who shouted, 'Do what he says. Don't touch that chimney-stack – it might fall at any moment. Get right away from it. Do you want to kill yourself?'

A Broken Leg and Annie goes Missing

The stack shook and swayed alarmingly, and brick dust and mortar showered down. Some local lads who had gathered were clinging to the top of the fence to watch the fun, while two housewives tut-tutted as they passed along the road on their way to the shops.

Brian, oblivious to everything except escape, thrust forward to swing himself round the stack and so into the adjoining house. He found a handhold on an exposed fireplace, paused for a moment, then with a quick movement leapt like a monkey onto the partition wall. In a deluge of masonry and black dust the fireplace dislodged itself and leant outwards at an alarming angle. From the stack, weakened by storms, rain and frost, came the sound of cracking brickwork. The topmost section was the narrowest and fell first, rushing past Brian's cowering body in a cloud of choking dust. Cracks started zigzagging in jerky movements throughout the entire structure as the fireplace shifted forward and finally fell. Brian took his chance and jumped off the partition wall with only split seconds to spare, landing awkwardly on a pile of bricks and rolling away clutching his leg. The last the onlookers saw was his flailing arms disappearing in a cloud of dust, broken timbers, masonry and chimney-pots.

Silence fell as the dust settled. After what seemed an eternity of waiting muffled curses and a stirring of loose rubble indicated that Brian was still alive. His filthy head rose from the debris as he struggled to escape from under the weight of bricks. Defiant to the last, he shouted, 'Don't just stand there gawping. Come and help me. My leg's killing me; I think it's broken.'

As they turned into the bottom of the road near their house, the memory and implications of their trip to the bombsite still reverberating in their minds, Chris and Tim knew that something serious had happened. Two neighbours were on the pavement talking earnestly, and as they approached one turned back through her gate and the other hurried off to her house, two doors down the road. As she disappeared she called out to Chris, 'Your mother's beside herself with worry. Annie's been missing all morning. Weren't you meant to be looking after her?'

7. Brian is caught in the bombed building

Chris mumbled something in reply, then turned to Tim. 'We're really in for it now. First the police, now this.' Hesitantly they went into the house.

'And where on earth have you two been?' asked Mother, pale-faced and her voice full of strain. 'Didn't I ask you to keep an eye on Annie while I did the ironing? Now look what's happened. It's simply not good enough. Christopher, you . . . you at your age should know better.' She paused, trying to control her anger and distress. The use of his full Christian name was always a bad sign. 'The police need to know the exact time you last saw her.'

'It was an hour or so after breakfast, say 9.30. She was in her pedal car at the top of the garden. We told her to come back to the house to be with you, and the last we saw of her was on the back steps.'

'Well, that was no help to me, was it? You knew I had the housework to do.' She paused. 'The neighbours are looking for her and so are the police, so you'd both better get back on your bikes and join in.'

Tim squirmed and looked up shyly. 'Can we have our dinner first?'

Their mother threw up her arms in despair and rushed from the room. 'All they ever think about is their stomachs!'

'You blithering idiot, why mention food?' Chris exploded, transferring his feelings of guilt onto Tim, whose eyes were already watering. 'We'll just make ourselves a sandwich.'

Glad to be away from the tensions of the house, the brothers freewheeled down the road following the pavements, guessing that Annie would not cross too many roads or go along the muddy lane at the bottom of their street. Tim was tired from his long ride earlier and all the excitement of the morning, and was now feeling weary and nervous. Near Moore's Garage they saw one of their mother's friends hanging out her washing. No, she had seen and heard nothing, but would keep her eyes peeled and would mention it to her neighbours.

The main road was quite busy, with cars, vans and buses passing each way.

Tim looked at Chris as they tried to make up their minds. 'She can't possibly have crossed that – and the pavement turns towards the town.'

'Perhaps she turned left up the hill. If so, she'd pass the shop at the top of our road.' Tim's idea cheered him up.

'So why's she not safely back at home? That hill's much too steep for her, and anyway she'd have been spotted by lots of people who know her. No, I reckon she went towards the town.'

So they crossed the traffic and took much the same route as they had earlier in the morning. They circled the old market square, where four of Chris's schoolfriends were fooling about on a bench. Chris explained their predicament, but again no one had seen anything. The two boys wondered where to go next.

'She might have got hungry and called at a sweetshop,' suggested Tim tentatively, aware that his ideas were often pooh-poohed by Chris.

'Don't be daft. What would she do for money?'

They looked up a few further streets but there was no sight of her. 'Time we were getting back,' Chris said glumly, but Tim's comment had given him an idea. They turned for home and Chris led the way past a small group of shops used regularly by their mother, a post office, butcher and grocer. Here the river split into two, crossed by a medieval causeway, with Mr Budden's grocery shop on the island in the middle.

'Morning, Master Chris. Are you well?' the friendly grocer greeted them. Tim climbed onto a sack of potatoes so that he could look down through a wide bay-window at the waving clumps of green waterweed in the river below. Over the exposed gravel patches he counted several trout.

'Not really, Mr Budden, thank you all the same. We've lost Annie.'

'Well, I'll pass the news on to all my customers and if they've heard anything I'll give you a ring.'

'Better ring Mrs Keeling next door. We're not on the phone yet.'

'Yes, of course, how silly of me.'

The boys pressed on, asking at two more shops before turning down a gravel track past Mr Moore's garage. He was in the workshop at the rear with his son John. They were changing the engine of an old MG sports car, soon to be John's.

'Hello, you two. What brings you here?' Chris explained the position yet again, and Mr Moore went into the showroom that faced the main road to ask if the salesman had seen anything. Tim gazed round the workshop in wonderment. An elderly mechanic was inspecting the exhaust system of a Morris 8, while a younger apprentice changed the tyres on a Humber Super Snipe. Puddles of spilt oil lay here and there covered in heaps of sawdust, leaving an acrid smell in the air. Outside were piles of old tyres and cracked windscreens. Tim was surprised to see pictures of naked women as the toilet door briefly opened and shut. Mr Moore laughed at his shocked expression.

'We used to have five young mechanics here, always up for a bit of fun. They're all in khaki now, mending tanks and lorries – two in North Africa with Monty, two others doing their training. They tell me Fred was killed in the retreat to Dunkirk. What a mess. Now all I'm left with is old Tom and a fifteen-year-old apprentice who's not got long before he's called up.' Mr Moore paused to reflect, then brightened up. 'But I've still got John here at weekends and holidays – useless as he is!' He winked at Chris and Tim as they climbed back onto their bikes. His son blew a raspberry at his father, and they all laughed.

Anxious about the reception they might receive, the boys returned home with nothing useful to report to their mother. They retreated quietly to their bedroom, Chris to continue a jig-saw puzzle and Tim to read. Mother cat, pregnant again, looked up from her favourite spot on Tim's bed, yawned and went back to sleep. Tim stretched out on his bed, tickled her with his socked feet and tried to lose himself in his book.

By mid-afternoon tension in the house was rising to breaking-point, and their mother went next door to share her troubles with Dorothy Keeling, fast becoming a close friend. Together they chewed over a few ideas. Was Annie unhappy at home? Did her brothers bully or tease her? Did they leave her out of their games? There was nothing obvious they could think of.

'I'd better get the boys their tea, though frankly they only deserve bread and water and to be sent straight to bed!'

'What a dreadful thing to say,' said Mrs Keeling in mock-horror. They both burst out laughing – the comment had broken the sombre atmosphere.

As Mrs Mason was about to leave the phone rang, and both women jumped at the sound. 'Yes, Mrs Keeling speaking . . .' She covered the mouthpiece with her hand. 'It's the police. They've got good news . . . Yes, by chance she's here now so I'll pass you over straight away.'

Annie had been spotted by a friend of theirs, Mrs Fleming, on her way back from the shops, more than two miles away on the other side of town. It was from the Flemings that the pedal car had been recently bought, so she had recognised it at once. She was surprised not to see any of the little girl's family with her and had called the police. Annie was exhausted but quite safe, though not able to tell the police very much about her expedition. They had felt it best for Mrs Fleming to return the child to her mother in person, just to speed things along a little; she would be there in a short time.

Once reunited with Annie, the release of worry and tension produced a flood of tears on her mother's part, her emotions overwhelmed with gratitude for all the support and help offered by her neighbours. Later on Mrs Keeling took charge. 'What you need, m'gal, is a stiff drink.' She went to a cabinet and poured out two generous whiskies. 'Soda water?'

'Actually I'd prefer a dash of lemonade.'

'What?' laughed Mrs Keeling. 'How to wreck a good drink in one easy movement!'

9
HETTY BRAKE AND A GASHED HEAD

'I'll be out today,' announced Mrs Mason over breakfast. 'The College is using its half-term break to carry out piano tests for the music students, and they want me to conduct examinations today and tomorrow. Miss Brake will keep an eye on you and look after Annie.' This was only a few days after the bomb-site incident – and Brian was still in hospital with complications to his broken leg. A residual tension hung in the air over Annie's little escapade; the boys were 'on probation.'

Chris looked at Tim and they smiled. They adored Miss Brake. She was a pleasantly rounded lady in her middle years who must have been attractive in her time. Boyfriend after boyfriend had been killed in the terrible battles of the First World War, two in one morning on the Somme. She, like so many other young women of her time, had remained single. She was outgoing, always cheerful, and prone to hoots of laughter when she would clap her hands over her mouth to stop her false teeth flying out. She chased balls energetically round the lawn till she was exhausted, by which time beads of perspiration glistened in the thriving moustache on her upper lip. She cheated at cards and had a natural affinity with younger people. 'The naughtier the better' was her motto.

At around ten o'clock she puffed her way up the back steps. 'Phew! Another hot day. What a lovely autumn we're having. Bound to suffer for it later, I daresay. Hello, you boys. What mischief have you been up to lately?' Tim opened his mouth to tell her all about Saturday, but was cut short by Chris. 'Nothing really. It's been a very boring weekend.'

'I can't believe that!' she laughed. 'A boring weekend with you two around? That's not possible.' She looked towards the boys' mother, who decided to say nothing; she would miss the bus if she didn't go soon.

'There's loads of cut bread for sandwiches if you go off somewhere. Thanks for helping me out, Miss B. You're a real brick.' Tim thought it curious to call someone a brick; it seemed a bit rude.

'So what'll we do?' asked Chris. 'Can we go fishing?'

'I don't see why not if Tim agrees.'

'Yes, whoopee! The Moat's good for fishing, or what about the Pools?'

'The Moat's no good – they're only tiddlers there. The Pools are much better, and we can sail our boats too. The White Bridge is no good any more, because the farmer's put a stop to it. He says we'll be caught by the river-keeper one day.'

'The Pools it is,' said Miss Brake. Of the three options this was the furthest, and in a resigned way she thought about the long bicycle ride ahead of her. Ah well, it was the boys' wishes that came first. 'Now you disappear for half an hour while I get the lunch ready.'

'Can I help?' asked Tim. 'I can boil the kettle and make up something to drink from the Eiffel Tower lemonade crystals if you like.'

The party assembled and set off. The boys tied their fishing rods to the cross-bars of their bicycles and put sandwiches and a drink in their saddle bags. Miss Brake, who was carrying a string bag that held the rest of the food as well as Annie's colouring book and dolly, strapped the little girl into the child's seat of their mother's old Sunbeam cycle. 'Make sure you've all got your sun hats. It'll get pretty hot out in the sun today.'

The lane was dry and dusty, and Chris was soon way out ahead with Tim shouting at him to slow down. Miss Brake wobbled alarmingly and struggled to keep up. 'Slow down,' she gasped, 'let's keep together.'

The blackbirds, thrushes and robins, whose songs had accompanied them on the way down the road, soon gave way to chaffinches and yellowhammers as they left the houses behind. They entered a long gravel footpath with trees on one side and cows grazing in the field on the other.

'Stop a moment, you two. I'm puffed, and this path is too narrow for me to cycle along safely. Annie's getting to be such a weight these days.'

Miss Brake slowly pushed the top-heavy bicycle along, getting her breath back and soaking in the gorgeous morning. Further up the path she could see that the boys, too, had stopped and seemed absorbed by something in the field. It was a cow giving birth: a white 'tennis-ball' had appeared under the cow's tail and was slowly getting larger. Chris decided to go and tell the farmer as the others settled down to watch. By now the cow was making soft lowing noises, which made the others stop grazing and look up at her. Minutes passed and Tim was getting anxious. Where was the farmer?

'It's all part of nature.' Miss Brake tried to dispel Tim's anxiety. 'She'll be all right.'

The cow looked slowly from side to side as what appeared to be a pair of hooves wrapped in a transparent film emerged. The cow made a short bellow and rolled onto its side, and the calf's head appeared.

'Mr Miller will look by when he gets in for lunch,' announced Chris, swerving up on his bike. The cow was now straining and bellowing in equal measures as at least half the body had appeared. With a final push and a wet flopping sound the calf slid out onto the grass, kicking its way out of the containing membrane. Its mother struggled round to face it, licking its nose and mouth. It coughed twice and tried to stand up on its wobbly legs as the mother cow licked its bright black shiny coat all over.

'Oh no!' cried Tim in disgust. 'Now it's eating all that stuff that came out with the calf!'

'I think we've seen enough,' laughed Miss Brake. 'You're not going to enjoy your lunch if you stay here much longer.'

Soon they were leaning over the wooden railings of White Bridge, peering down into the clear water to look for trout and grayling.

'Here, Tim. Don't make a sound. Look down there just by that muddy patch. See it?'

'No, can't see anything.'

'There's a small jack pike there, idiot. About three pounds I should think – quite a nice fish.' Close to the bank, looking like a greeny-brown log and with only its dorsal and tail fins moving to keep station in the current, the pike's back was dappled by the reflections of ripples in the midday sunlight. Chris felt compelled to show off more of his knowledge. 'They can grow up to ten or twelve pounds in this tributary but much larger in the main river. The river-keeper was telling me about a twenty-eight-pounder caught on a spinner last year. Its teeth made a real mess of the fisherman's hand getting the hooks out.'

Once on their way again they passed the old smithy, with its assortment of farm machinery long since deemed unrepairable, abandoned outside and overgrown with weeds. From inside the workshop flashes and sparks lit up the ceiling as the smithy welded a set of ploughshares. Soon afterwards they passed a humpy bridge, its stream leading to a battlemented Victorian house surrounded by a mass of turgid unmoving water, the Moat. Then past the baker's by the village green and so along a gravelly farm track to the Pools. In this section of the valley a series of eight streams had been dug to create water meadows, designed to provide the first flush of spring grass for the cows to eat after their winter incarceration in sheds. Where the cows had walked through these streams over countless years, shallow pools had formed. The level of the water in the pools was controlled by sluice-gates, and this was vital for the boys' enjoyment. If the water was deep, a pool was best for fishing; if it was shallow it was ideal for paddling and sailing their yachts.

Chris and Tim threw their bikes against a fence and crossed the first footbridge excitedly.

What was the water-level in the various pools? The last three were virtually flooded and much too deep for fishing, paddling or even for the cows to cross. Clearly these were being used to move excess water quickly down the valley, but the first three looked promising.

Miss Brake had stopped at the first pool and was unfastening Annie from her seat. 'Oh my!' she gasped. 'I'm quite worn out. Where you two get your energy from defeats me. I'm staying here with Annie, so come back when you want your dinner.' She rigged up her umbrella to act as a sunshade and settled down, as Annie pulled out her jam jar and wandered down to the pool. The water's edge was chewed up by the cows' hooves and covered by an evil green slimy mud, which soon transferred itself to her little blue gumboots. Her jam jar bobbed about in the water but would not sink. 'Go and give her a hand,' said Miss Brake.

'We're trying to sort out the rigging on our yachts. It's all got jumbled up.' The boys were not in the mood to be helpful. Miss Brake sighed and went to Annie's assistance, showing her how to cast the jam jar into deeper water. Annie pulled it out almost at once, giggling with pleasure. The pot was full of muddy water, a sprig of weed and a caddis-fly larva. She emptied its contents onto the path and shrieked in horror as the insect dragged its scaly body towards her. Miss Brake did her best to distract her with the dolly and colouring book.

By now the boys had launched their yachts and were paddling around pushing them into the intermittent breeze that fanned in bursts across the pool, trying to stop the water splashing over into their gumboots. Peace reigned.

For an hour or so all went well. The hooks and eyes through which the rigging passed sometimes became loose and had to be bashed back into the wood with a stone. Often a yacht got too far out into the main current and started drifting alarmingly towards the footbridge and away downstream, perhaps to be lost for ever. This always caused panic.

'Grab it quick, Tim. You're nearest. Get a move on, you fool.' Tim floundered out of the pool, ran onto the footbridge and threw himself onto his stomach. Just in time he grabbed the mast as it bobbed its way underneath. As the breeze turned gusty it started to blow the boats over – and finally the boys lost interest in their yachts.

'Did you have a good time?' asked Miss Brake, pulling sandwiches and apples from her bag. 'Annie was frightened by a creepy-crawly she found in the river. What did we do next?'

Annie thought for a minute. 'We went for a walk, and Miss Brake put her foot in a stinky cowpat and lots of horrible orange flies flew out.'

'I wasn't thinking of that exactly,' said Miss Brake, wishing to forget the incident. 'What else did we see on our walk?'

Another pause as Annie thought for a minute. 'A tin can with paint in it? Oh, I know . . . a fisher-king, all blue and green.'

'Well done, dear. It was a kingfisher. You're learning fast.'

Chris and Tim looked suspiciously into their sandwiches: ugh, peanut butter. They were followed by swiss roll and apples from the garden. Dinner took all of seven minutes to eat.

'Let's try a bit of fishing,' suggested Chris. 'Perhaps the levels will have dropped in those deep pools. If so there may be some whoppers in there.' They pulled up turves to find worms, and threaded them, wriggling, onto their hooks. Tim always felt a pang of sorrow at this necessary but unkind deed. Chris risked the deeper pools and after some time caught three grayling. Tim preferred the quieter water, and after changing from worms to small pellets of bread he succeeded in catching several minnows and two small dace.

The afternoon wore on enjoyably. Tiring of fishing, Tim held Annie's hand and together they paddled in the warm water of the shallowest pool. They turned over stones, laughing at the miller's thumbs that wriggled out of their fingers as they grabbed at them, and gazing in wonderment at the vivid colours of a stickleback they had caught in a jam jar. A heron flying overhead changed direction suddenly as it spotted the children below.

It was around teatime and they were getting ready to go home when the accident happened. The boys had taken off their boots to dry them out in the sun, and against orders they made a last dash for the pool and started splashing each other wildly.

'Stop that at once. Come on out *now*!' Miss Brake was getting exasperated as she watched things getting out of hand. Chris advanced on Tim, gleefully scooping up handfuls of water and soaking his shirt and trousers. Retreating in the face of this onslaught, Tim stumbled over a hidden brick and lost his footing, falling heavily against the concrete pillar of the footbridge. Chris's whoop of victory quickly changed to concern as Tim lay for several moments stretched out in the water before struggling to sit up, clutching at his head. Blood oozed through his fingers and ran in flowing streaks down his wet face, splashing onto his shirt. Chris rushed to his side.

Hetty Brake and a Gashed Head

'My goodness! Whatever has happened?' Miss Brake, packing away the picnic things and trying to keep Annie occupied at the same time, called out urgently, 'Chris, help him out at once. I asked you not to go in the water again.'

Tim, the immediate shock wearing off, was starting to feel the pain of the cut and was becoming frightened by the sight of all the blood. Feeling dizzy and sick he flopped down onto the grass.

Miss Brake came over to inspect the wound and, thinking quickly, mopped at it with her headscarf and told Chris to get some clean water in a jam jar. 'But wash it out first.' She found it impossible to staunch the flow of blood coursing through Tim's hair from the nasty gash in the back of his head. This caused Tim to start sobbing, quickly followed by Annie which added to the general sense of drama. 'Chris, you'd better try and find someone who can drive Tim to a doctor or to hospital. You could try the baker or the blacksmith. When he's feeling a bit better we'll walk up the lane to the road and wait for you there. Now Annie, will you stop that noise. Tim's going to be perfectly all right.' Secretly she was extremely worried.

Chris pedalled off as fast as he could and knocked at several doors by the village green without success. The blacksmith switched off his welding gear and considered the problem. 'I can't really break off at the moment, because there's a customer coming to collect this job any minute now. But I'll ring the vicar. Monday's always a quiet day for the clergy, isn't it?' He winked at Chris. 'After all, they only work one day a week.' He chuckled to himself at his joke, but Chris was too anxious to find it amusing.

Coming back from the phone, the blacksmith said, 'The vicar's wife will be here in a few minutes. She's visiting parishioners in the hospital later today so she's happy to help out.'

Chris pedalled back to the track and looked out for the others. A little way along he came across the sorry-looking group, with Tim slumped in the hedge, his head in his hands. He had tried to push his bike along but had given up when he felt as if he was going to faint. He was finding it difficult to focus and had been sick twice. Miss Brake knew that these were not good signs.

The vicar's wife Mrs Alderson had already reversed the car off the road by the time Chris rejoined his brother. Before her marriage she had been a nurse. 'Just keep him talking,' she said, as Tim was helped onto the back seat. 'We'll sort the bikes out later. Hetty, you get into the front seat with Annie, and I'll drop you off first. You need to get her back to her mother as soon as possible or she'll start worrying.'

Less than a quarter of an hour later the car pulled up at the casualty department of the hospital. Tim was seen by a doctor who removed the sodden, blood-clotted dressing carefully and sterilised the wound. Chris watched, intrigued.

'That'll need a few stitches,' murmured the doctor, peering closely at Tim's matted hair. 'I'll give you a couple of local injections to take away the pain. I'm afraid this will hurt for a few moments until the anaesthetic takes effect.' The gash was stitched and bandaged, making Tim look like an Indian fakir. Chris had to snigger.

After a short discussion, Mrs Alderson and the doctor decided that Tim's symptoms might be more serious than at first thought. After all, there was clearly the possibility of concussion, so they decided he should spend a night in hospital under observation. Upstairs, in a general ward, a bed had been prepared surrounded by a screen so he could change into pyjamas. Chris accompanied him in the lift, to help calm his unease as the nurse fussed over him and joked with them both. 'We're putting you next to another young lad who's had a nasty fall. He's got his broken leg in traction.'

They waited in anticipation as the screens were removed, only to cry out in groans of amused surprise and recognition. Even the battle-scarred Tim, poorly as he was, managed a half-smile and a chuckle. His fellow neighbour was none other than the dreaded Brian Priddy.

10
AUNT ELLIE AND A TEA-TIME RITUAL

'Now you've got to be on your best behaviour for a few days because your father's sister, Aunt Ellie, is coming to stay. She'll be sleeping in his bedroom while she's here.' The boys sensed from their mother's demeanour that their aunt was not much liked. What a shame their father was still abroad and unable to entertain her.

Aunt Ellie imposed a heavy hand on the children right from the start. She was extremely bossy and corrected them regularly, especially at mealtimes, when she criticised their table manners and slovenly speech. 'I notice you don't always say "please" and "thank you". It's only good manners to do such a simple thing. And why do you speak in such a sloppy way?' She waited for a response.

'Probably because it's *our* house and we do and say what we please!' muttered Chris under his breath. Tim giggled, and Annie joined in. Their mother, washing up dishes at the sink, partly overheard the remark and could not help smiling.

Aunt Ellie scowled. 'It's extremely rude to mutter, and as for the remark itself, Christopher, I shall pretend I didn't hear it.' Chris had the grace to blush as the meal continued. 'And Tim, your mother tells me you play the piano. How lovely. I hope you'll let me hear you before I go on Thursday.' Tim felt himself shrinking inside with a dull feeling of fear. This was the one thing he dreaded – playing the piano in front of others. Roll on the day of her departure, thought the boys, as of one mind!

Somehow Thursday afternoon came, and still he had not played for Aunt Ellie. Her things were packed and her taxi was due at any moment.

She made a final stern ultimatum, but Tim shrank deeper into his chair and pulled the book he was reading closer to his face. Anxiety was taking control of him.

'Be a good boy, dear,' coaxed his mother. 'The relatives in Yorkshire are always asking how you're getting on with your music.' Tim wanted to please his mother, and was on the point of going over to the piano stool to start when the feeling of dread overwhelmed him. He hesitated.

'Well, I'm disgusted. What a rude, ungrateful little boy you are. Is it really too much to ask of you? You're a disgrace to your brave father who's facing who-knows-what dangers overseas.'

In a surge of uncontrollable misery and suppressed fury Tim rushed from the sitting room and into the bathroom. He locked the door and sat on the toilet seat, shaking, too emotionally overcome for tears. For a time he was safe; no one would bother him now. He started to calm down.

'Tim, *do* come out. Aunt Ellie's taxi will be here at any moment to take her to the station and she needs to spend a penny before her train journey.' She was trying her best to cajole him out of the bathroom, but he sensed a feeling of power slowly rising within him: the tables were being turned; he was gaining the upper hand. He sat tight for a few moments in silence, waiting.

'Coming, Mum, just doing a poo.' A long pause ensued. There was a knock at the front door, followed by a flurry of activity as doors were opened and shut and footsteps went up and down the hallway.

'Now that's quite enough, Tim. You're just being difficult.' His mother's angry and exasperated voice came from close against the bathroom door. 'The taxi's here and you must come out and say goodbye to your aunt.'

By now a sense of sheer devilment had came over him. Tim ripped four sheets of loo paper noisily from the hook on the wall. 'Sorry, Mum. Just wiping my bottom. Won't be long now.' He craned his head forward listening to the final goodbyes, the sound of the car pulling away up the street and his mother, Chris and Annie returning to the house, laughing with relief at Aunt Ellie's departure. This was the exact moment he chose to leave the bathroom, announcing proudly, 'All finished now, Mum.'

Aunt Ellie and a Tea-Time Ritual

✻ ✻ ✻

The school holidays had come round again and Mother made the usual announcement on the first day. 'I've arranged your visit to the dentist for tomorrow, ten o'clock. And tea with the aunts this Sunday afternoon.' The double helping of bad news was met with groans. She knew that the visit to the dentist with his slow-grinding drill, lack of local anaesthetics, and worst of all the dreaded gas for extractions, wrecked their enjoyment of the holidays until it was over.

The regular three times a year trip to the aunts was something of a mixed blessing, since apart from the splendid tea there was always the added bonus of the ten shilling note which was given to each, thanked for effusively, and then put straight into their Post Office savings accounts by their mother. These visits had settled into a monotonously predictable pattern. First there were two bus rides out into the country to the gaunt, cavernous and cold house, inside which the two elderly ladies rattled like peas in a pod. Then there was a sinking feeling as they knocked on the front door, in anticipation of three hours of stilted and boring conversation.

'Oh, how lovely to see you both. Are you well? How smart and grown up you look these days – quite the young gentlemen! Did you have a good journey? And is your mother keeping well?'

The monologue continued without cease, leaving little space for an answer. The younger aunt, dressed from head to foot in black, led them into the sitting room where her elder sister, also in black, sat quietly in an armchair by a coal fire, her back protected from draughts by a Japanese screen. The room was oppressively gloomy, its dark blue and brown velvet curtains and embossed wallpaper dampening the boys' spirits. The dark Victorian furniture and heavy mahogany dining table, which occupied the centre of the room, cast an overpowering feeling of times long past.

'Come and sit next to me, Tim, and tell me all about your progress at school. Are you doing any new subjects? Are you in any teams? And how is your piano-playing coming along?' Pulling a straight-backed chair with a hard upholstered seat nearer to the fire, he winced at the ghastly memory of another aunt's recent visit. The questions continued remorselessly. He struggled to reply.

'Well give them a chance to answer, Cecily!' the older aunt rebuked her sister.

An awkward silence followed. The only sounds came from the muffled crackling of the fire and the relentless ticking of the grandfather clock in the hall. Tim glanced apprehensively towards Chris, who launched bravely into an account of his term's activities. Yes, thank you, he was doing well, and had been selected for the second rugby fifteen. He had come second in his class in a Maths test and was now learning French. '*Je suis, tu es, il est, nous sommes, vous êtes, ils sont*,' he gabbled, concentrating hard and rattling the words off parrot-fashion.

'My, how interesting! You *are* clever. And what does that mean?' Aunt Rose looked towards him encouragingly.

Chris's face changed suddenly from pride to embarrassment as he blushed and said, 'I'm not quite sure.'

Sensing an awkward moment had developed, Tim said, 'Mother cat has had four kittens, and the second night she brought them one by one into my bed. It's lovely. They tickle me and keep my feet warm.' He paused, as Aunt Cecily looked surprised and Chris frowned in his direction. He decided to change tack a little. 'And Ginger-Tom cut his tongue badly, licking out a sardine tin, and we had to take him to the vet's. He takes ages to drink his milk, now that there's not much of his tongue left.'

A long pause developed as a piece of coal made a hissing noise and puffed out a wisp of smoke.

'Thank goodness the worst of the winter's over now. I *do* love the spring,' said Aunt Rose in a vacant sort of way, gazing dreamily at the fire. 'The trees will soon be covered in leaves again.'

'Don't be so ridiculous,' scolded Aunt Cecily, trying to keep a hold on her sister's increasing senility. 'We haven't even had Christmas yet. I think it's time for tea.'

In the summer months the boys were allowed to go into the garden for a short breath of fresh air before tea. At its far end beyond the lawn and hedges was a small tributary of the main river, a shallow and muddy stream overhung by willow trees where a few sad-looking minnows and small dace spiralled in circles in the turgid water. However welcome this escape from the house was, it hardly compared with their river at home and they could not even consider doing any fishing. And anyway, they didn't dare get any mud on their shoes or trousers. In winter even this short diversion into a world of reality was denied them.

'Come and sit down, it's all ready.' The strangely ill-matched quartet settled round the table. 'You pour, will you, Cis? My hands aren't what they used to be,' Aunt Rose sighed ruefully.

The tea service was silver, the elegant cups and saucers had tiny spoons at their sides, and table-mats and napkins indicated where each person should sit. The table overflowed with sandwiches, bread and butter, two sorts of jam in dishes with spoons, biscuits and three sorts of cake. The boys never saw anything like this at home and tucked in heartily. They were encouraged to eat as much as they liked.

'Could I have orangeade, please?' asked Tim shyly, preferring it to tea.

'Of course, dear.' His aunt filled a glass and passed it over. Even drinking out of a glass was a novelty – at home they used jam jars.

As Tim stretched out his arm his shirt cuff caught the handle of his knife, which spun upwards and dropped into his lap, leaving a dark purple jammy smear on his white and recently ironed shirt front. As he glanced down in consternation his hand knocked against the glass of orangeade, and it spilt heavily onto the tablecloth. His aunt quickly lifted its embroidered edge and slipped a tea towel underneath to protect the table's polished surface from the spreading liquid. Tim looked mortified.

'Don't worry, dear. Accidents will happen.'

These kind words went some way towards alleviating Tim's embarrassment. Would he now forfeit the customary 'one shilling for good table-manners' that was always presented to each of them at the end of the meal? This had never happened before!

In the silence that followed the grandfather clock struck five times. Its resonant chimes echoed hollowly round the empty hallway, mingling with the fire's crackling and the sound of a distant car. Tim counted the chimes as he silently ticked off the seconds of his life slipping remorselessly away, increasingly aware of his own mortality. Only one more hour of this stultifying boredom to go before they were back on the bus again and heading towards real life once more.

His eyes wandered idly round the room, at the oval-framed mirrors, at the paintings of flowers in vases and cottages by streams, and at the sepia photographs of tall, dark-suited gentlemen.

'Come and sit by the fire till it's time for your bus,' said Aunt Rose as Cecily removed some of the tea things to the kitchen. 'It's been such a long winter, but I expect you enjoy riding your bikes now the spring has come again.' She lapsed into silence: the boys, mystified, said nothing.

Suddenly Tim had a brainwave. 'Thank you for the armchair you sent over on Reg Hardiman's lorry. It's really comfortable. And we've all christened it.' He beamed with pride at this interesting contribution to the conversation.

Aunt Cecily, joining them, said, 'Oh, I am pleased. And what have you decided to call it?'

Blushing, as he realised the implications of what he had just said, Tim was at a loss for words. Chris offered a lame explanation, which sounded very unconvincing. For when the chair had been brought into the sitting room after a beans on toast supper the boys had indeed 'christened' the chair. In turns, amid screams of laughter, they had vented their foul wind into its soft fabric, producing blasts of evil-smelling air. Even Mother, knitting by the fire, had been forced to smile at the fun they were having. Only the cat objected, scratching at the door to be let out.

11
THE CAMP, HOSPITAL AND A GERMAN BOMBER

It wasn't long before Brian Priddy, now recovered from his broken leg, called round at the house again. His approach followed the familiar pattern; a pale freckled face under a tousled mop of ginger hair that thrust itself round the corner of the house, followed by a hoarse whisper to attract Tim or Chris's attention.

Tim spotted him, and nodded. 'Mum, I'm just off on my bike for a bit. Is that OK?'

'Yes, dear. Be back for dinner, won't you. Where are you off to?'

'Oh, just mooching around . . . you know . . .'

Released for the morning, Tim joined Brian – who was doing wheelies on his bike with David and Peter Keeling from next door. They swooped round each other, forming graceful arcs in the road, occasionally colliding with each other and falling off. Soon bored, they wondered what to do next.

'We could go down the lane to the farm,' suggested Tim.

'It might be muddy after last night's rain,' added Peter.

'We could always try the air-raid shelter,' said Chris, who had just joined them with a flurry of screeching brakes. Chris was naturally drawn to the activities of the more 'grown-up' members of the local community, both boys and girls, which took place at the air-raid shelter. The younger boys showed a marked lack of interest in this idea.

Brian took charge. 'Hey, I know what. My dad says a new camp's opened on Overleigh Down. It's full of Italian prisoners of war who were captured in North Africa. Let's go and see them.' This idea appealed to the boys' imagination and they agreed to give it a go. Tim was uncertain, especially when young Peter Keeling quietly pushed his bike back through his front gate, but summoned up the courage to join them. The boys cycled off up the road, chattering noisily.

Their route took them at first along the main road to the south coast, which was now increasingly occupied by military traffic. Bright red buses and black saloon cars wove their way as best they could between the columns of khaki-coloured, slow-moving vehicles. Tim need not have worried about keeping up with the older boys: Brian's bike was old with rattling mudguards and a stiff chain, and he laboured along in the rear, complaining bitterly.

After a short distance they crossed the road and skirted a large chalk-pit into the first of two sunken green lanes, ancient trackways that had been enlarged over the years by the wheels of farmers' wagons. Nowadays these lanes were stopping places for gypsies and tinkers, usually cheerful people, though not always, who wore colourful clothing and sat outside their decorated caravans chattering and carving wooden pegs. They fascinated Tim, though he was upset after one group had moved on to find a pile of sheep bones under the hedge nearby, no doubt an unwitting gift from the local farmer.

Well away from the road now, Tim was conscious of the chaffinches and skylarks singing in the warm sunshine, and the bees and insects humming around the elderflower blossom. Hawthorn bushes were in their full springtime foliage.

The boys struggled on up the uneven chalk track, their tyres slipping off lumps of chalk and damp turf. At last, where two lanes crossed, they encountered the first of a series of chain-link fences with inward-turned tops, entangled with several strands of barbed wire. At the top of the down they could see rows of brown wooden huts, with groups of men standing about, chatting idly. The boys pushed their bikes further up the hill to where two soldiers in khaki uniforms were smoking, their rifles leaning against the wire. One held his cigarette behind his back as the boys approached.

'Wotcher!' he said cheerfully. 'Out for a ride, then?' He cast his eye inquisitively over the group, conscious of the need for security.

'Er . . . yes, just passing through. Taking in a bit of fresh air . . . having a look around.' Brian's reply, as he looked at the ground and shuffled his feet, immediately appeared evasive. Why did he always sound suspicious, thought Tim?

'My dad's a doctor in the army,' said David brightly. 'We heard about this camp and thought we'd come and have a look. Where are the prisoners from?' His open and friendly manner broke the ice, and the other soldier explained.

'They're Italians. First they were squeezed at one end of North Africa by the Auk and Monty and at the other by Ike and Patton, and then they were beaten in Sicily and southern Italy as well. They're in dead trouble, giving themselves up in droves. As a fighting force they won't last much longer.'

The first soldier laughed. 'They're mostly behind wire somewhere out east, as there aren't enough empty troop ships to bring them back to England. Mind you, they're a friendly lot, peasants rather than real fighters. All they want to do is volunteer for outside work and earn themselves a few extra bob.'

'Surely they want to escape,' said Tim, thinking of the comic books he had read.

'Lor' bless you, no,' the soldier spluttered with laughter. 'Once they've been caught that's it. They don't want to fight again, do they? Already lots are out on parole, working on farms or as butlers and gardeners in the posh houses around here. I'll be surprised if lots don't go back after the war to their ruined homes and a life of poverty, but decide to stay here.'

Tim pondered on these things, and saying goodbye to the soldiers he moved on to watch a football game between the prisoners further up the hill. Suddenly the ball came winging its way through the air and bounced off the fence. Three sweating men, shouting in a strange language, charged after it and booted it back, laughing. One lingered by the fence when he saw the boys and spoke to them in flowing Italian. Tim and David, unable to understand, shrugged their shoulders, smiling at the friendly prisoner as they climbed back on their bikes.

But Brian yelled out, 'Push off, you eyetie wop, you spaghetti-eating fool! Go back where you came from, idiot!'

The man looked surprised at first, then hurt, and let out a torrent of abuse, screaming at Brian with his fists clenched. All the pent-up anger at his capture and imprisonment was vented onto this insolent, worthless

English boy who was cruelly flaunting his freedom. The commotion alerted the guards, who quickly advanced towards Brian. Better get out fast, he thought, as he pedalled off after the others. Tim wondered again why Brian always managed to cause trouble and make a fool of himself. After all, he was a nice enough chap at heart.

The road back towards town passed a small military hospital, close to the road. Patients were sunning themselves on beds pushed outside, and called out to the boys, attracting their attention by waving chocolate and chewing gum. Many had bandaged heads, shoulders or arms, while others had their legs suspended by ropes and pulleys: all were cheerful and vociferous. The nurses did not seem to mind as Tim and the others swung round in the road, came in past the sentry and joined them: keeping these young and active men occupied during their convalescence was a continual problem.

'Are you Yanks?' Brian asked in his usual blunt and slightly aggressive way. He had noticed the American flag at the entrance gate.

'We most certainly are,' said a negro, whose bandaged arm was propped up on a pile of pillows. 'And, hey, you've got a lot of balls just barging in here without so much as a by-your-leave.' While saying this he picked up a Hershey chocolate bar with his other hand, which Brian accepted at once. 'Matron must be getting soft in her old age; she'd normally skin you alive!' These comments were delivered within her easy hearing while she was adjusting another patient's bedding. Brian had never seen a black man before, and eyed him with some suspicion. He wasn't too sure about the taste of the dark-coloured chocolate either.

'Why are you here?' asked David, who was developing an interest in all matters concerning the war.

'We're all American airmen, crew-members of those big B-17s you see flying over here. Flying Fortresses they're called – best bombers in the world. Crew of eleven, and seven of those are gunners. We raid industrial targets during daylight hours from thirty thousand feet, and with our new bomb-sight we can hit a pickle-barrel every time.' Loud coughing and the blowing of raspberries followed these boastful remarks.

'Hitler had better watch out now we're here.'

'With us the war's as good as won.'

8. *The boys chat to wounded Americans*

'You limeys may as well stay at home. Leave it all to Uncle Sam and President Roosevelt!'

A quiet airman near David explained that this was an American hospital, which took wounded airmen from the casualty wards on airfields for further treatment and convalescence. They were mostly grateful that they were out of the war and would probably be sent back home when they had recovered. So many of their friends had died in the skies over Germany.

Tim plucked up courage to speak. 'My mother comes up here sometimes. We live over there.' He pointed towards the houses by the main road. 'I think she comes to chat with you and keep you cheerful. Our dad's overseas as well.'

'What's her name?'

'Mrs Mason.'

'Why, that must be our Mary. She reads books to those who can't see properly and if we ask really nicely she plays the battered old piano in the main ward. She's pretty good, even though she's fairly well stuck on those old classical things. It's the devil of a job to get her to give us a bit of ragtime or play a few show tunes!'

This brought renewed interest from the airmen, who asked the nurse to bring out a cake from their Red Cross parcels. 'These kids look as though they could use a bit of fattening up!' This remark was greeted with laughter by the other airmen, and soon the boys were digging in to large slices of the richest fruitcake they had ever tasted.

Suddenly Tim caught sight of the clock on the hospital wall. 'Gosh! Look at the time. We're meant to be back for dinner.'

Waving their thanks, the boys pedalled home and stopped outside their house. Brian Priddy gave Tim a surreptitious nudge as he partially revealed two packets of Lucky Strike cigarettes in his pocket.

'Oh no. Don't tell me you pinched their cigarettes – after all their kindness.' Brian had the grace to blush, but Tim felt sick.

Chris came panting into the kitchen one day, exhausted from pedalling hard. 'David Keeling says there's a Jerry bomber parked in the market-place. It's been put there so that people can donate money to build more Spitfires. He says you can even go inside it.' This was particularly exciting for Tim, who was developing a real interest in aircraft.

The boys jumped on their bikes and rode into town, where they both noticed a large increase in military traffic. At one of the medieval gates leading into the cathedral precinct a stray lorry had lost its way and had tried to turn under the archway. It was now firmly wedged under the fourteenth-century stonework, and cracks had started to develop. The front tyres had been deflated, but the stonework had simply settled onto the cab as the driver tried to reverse out. Police and military personnel were in the middle of a heated discussion about the best solution to the problem, and a van had arrived with scaffolding poles to prevent a possible collapse.

'Let's get on to the market-place,' said Chris. 'We can come back later to see what's happened here.'

Occupying pride of place in the centre of the square was a Dornier 17, painted black for night raiding, with black and white crosses standing out starkly on wings and fuselage. On its twin tailplanes a small white swastika had been painted. These twin rudders seemed hardly large or strong enough to control the plane's movement and direction, placed as they were at the very end of a long, thin, tapering body.

Several air cadets were helping to control the crowds, keeping them back behind metal barriers, while an elderly Air Force officer, too old for active service, was holding forth to interested onlookers. 'Yes, this is a Dornier 217, the most common development of the Do 17. Apparently the pilot lost his way in bad weather on a raid over Bristol or Cardiff – we're not sure which – and when he found himself over a fair-sized stretch of water he assumed he was over the English Channel. Low on fuel, he spotted an airfield just before dawn and landed. Imagine his surprise when he found himself surrounded by a crowd of RAF erks at St Mawgan in Cornwall – silly bleeder had been over the Bristol Channel all the time! They've put this aircraft through its paces at the Farnborough Experimental Aircraft Establishment and reckon they've found out all there is to know, so now it's out on general display to raise money.'

'Did his bombs hit the target?' asked Tim.

'No. He dropped them in the sea once he was lost. They often do that. Or they panic and drop them on any light they see. That's why the black-out is so important. Of course our night-fighters are putting paid to them as well.'

Tim wandered under the cavernous black wing and looked into the Plexiglas nose-covering of the aircraft. What would it feel like to be stretched out on the floor with the searchlights flashing in your eyes, peering down onto houses, docks, factories and railways, and only the thinnest of aluminium to protect you from the shrapnel of bursting shells or the ripping of bullets from fighters? Yet apparently normal young men on both sides were enduring this day after day and night after night.

And what about the cost of all these complicated machines? Surely it must be possible to make ten or even twenty cars for the price of one of these sophisticated pieces of engineering. And what if it was shot down on its very first flight? What a terrible waste. Tim wondered how Britain, America, Russia and Germany could possibly afford the expense of running a war. Wouldn't they run out of money soon?

Nearby, a crowd had gathered around bits of old wings, tailplanes, engine parts, goggles, uniforms and cockpit instruments, gathered from crashed German aircraft and being sold off to souvenir hunters to support the war effort. A large black cross and smaller swastika were attracting the most attention and the highest prices as a local auctioneer drummed up further trade, his clerk standing next to him making a note of the sales. Tim couldn't help laughing at the auctioneer's ribald comments about Adolf Hitler, Goering and the other Nazis. It all seemed to encourage the onlookers to part with their money.

Losing interest, the boys returned to the lorry, which had been pulled out from under the arch by a recovery vehicle and was having its front tyres reinflated. Soldiers and drivers were sitting about on the pavement or leaning against their cabs, chatting. Temporary scaffolding was being tightened into position under the watchful eye of the cathedral architect. And as if there wasn't already enough confusion at this awkward junction, never of course intended for motor vehicles, a Queen Mary transport lorry was trying to negotiate the corner with an entire dismantled Hurricane on board. They watched for some minutes, then headed for home, pausing only when they spotted a small gaggle of youths near the entrance of an air-raid shelter.

Running underground in a zigzag pattern to minimise injuries in the event of a direct hit, the shelter had been built at the start of the war but was used only rarely. Its heavy metal entrance door was normally kept shut, but the local youngsters knew how to force it open. The boys saw a dim light flickering inside, and watched as older boys emerged, smirking and giggling amongst themselves. Curious, Tim questioned some younger boys standing nearby, but they either shrugged their shoulders or looked embarrassed and shuffled their feet. Chris, who had gone to find out what was going on, came back scoffing.

'Dirty beggars!' he said. 'They've got Sandra Pelly and Zoë Wilkinson in there, doing a bit of fiddling about – you know.' Tim wasn't sure exactly what his brother meant but thought he should find out. Chris was already quite a one with the girls and had no need for this sort of nonsense. 'I'm off,' he said. 'See you later.'

Tim approached the shelter in some trepidation and bumped into Brian Priddy. He *would* be there, wouldn't he, right in the thick of it.

'Got a penny or two on you?' he enquired.

'No such luck,' replied Tim, not quite telling the truth.

'Pity,' said Brian. 'Sandra'll let you have a quick look for a penny, and Zoë goes even further for tuppence!'

Tim started to blush, overcome with indecision. This was the chance of a lifetime; all it needed was a bit of nerve. But instead, cursing himself for his cowardice, he jumped on his bike and pedalled thoughtfully home.

12
A DROWNING, AN ACCIDENT AND A FATAL ILLNESS

The summer came early that year, with a particularly hot spell in May; the days passed in a blaze of sunshine and warmth. Tim spent much of his free time at White Bridge Farm, where Mr Tillman allowed him to fish in his back garden, away from the eyes of the river-keeper. He knew that Tim only caught small roach and chub and would not be taking any large fish out of the river. He had palled up with the eldest son, Hugh, who helped his father on the farm, driving tractors and carrying bales and sacks of corn. The boys often explored the barns together, chasing chickens and tickling the pigs in their pens. Most exciting, and risky, was teasing the bull as it stood morosely in its shed, tied up by a ring in its nose to a large bolt in the wall. It stamped its feet and bellowed when it got really cross. But what Tim enjoyed most was when Hugh took him up-river in the punt. This flat-bottomed boat was used by the river men to cut weeds and also to stun the fish by electrocution, so they could extract the carnivorous pike to be killed and return the game fish to the river alive.

'We're off to the cattle market,' shouted Mr Tillman. 'Hugh isn't coming so he'll be around all day if you want him.'

Tim nodded, waving, and turned back to his float bobbing wildly in the fast-moving current as Hugh wandered up behind him.

'You'll never catch anything here. It's too shallow and there are only tiddlers. Go down under the willows where the punt is. It's deeper and there are usually some good-sized fish. We've put an old oil drum there to catch crayfish – we found about a dozen lurking in there last week.' Hugh was four years older than Tim and knew all about the river.

Tim looked up at him hopefully. 'Any chance of a go in the punt?' he asked.

Hugh laughed; he knew exactly what Tim liked doing.

They pushed the front of the punt out into the river as Hugh undid the rope, and both jumped aboard. The current soon took control. 'Go on, shove the pole in quick . . . near the front. We're swinging round.' The river was quite deep here and the weight of the water was almost too much for Tim to push against, but he managed. Hugh climbed over the three bench seats and took up position at the back, thrusting strongly with his pole. 'Fend off the bank . . . keep her away from those reeds . . . watch out for that dead tree-trunk.' He kept up a steady stream of commands as they moved up through the garden where the going was tough – the current strongest and the water shallowest.

They struggled under the two old yew trees that met in the middle of the river, swiping their faces with the branches as they crouched low, trying to avoid them. Next came the small front garden with its neatly bricked banks, ideal for small children to leap off into the shallow water below. Many a hot afternoon had been spent there, as young relatives of the Tillmans together with Tim and Chris and various other local children splashed about and climbed in and out of an old tractor inner tube that bounced about on the water.

Once under the white bridge that gave the farm its name, and carefully avoiding the hard calcium stalactites, which had oozed out from the lime-rich brickwork over many years, they looked upstream towards the distant town. It was not long before the rhythmic action of punting, the sound of ripples lapping on the punt's side and the warmth of the sun on their arms and faces worked their magic, and the boys' chatter petered out. A gentle breeze carried small white clouds across the sky, and the wash caused by the punt's steady progress lapped against the reeds at the river's edge. This disturbed coots and moorhens, and caused water voles to bob up and down in the ripples before they disappeared underwater with a sudden plop.

The river deepened and took them under a thick line of very old willows, whose cracked and broken branches trailed down into the water, their tangled roots snatching and scraping at the sides of the punt as they passed. Underneath, deeply protected, were the dark holts of otters, long since abandoned for wilder stretches of the river away from the presence of humans. Smaller holes were the homes of water-voles and kingfishers. In the trees above willow warblers sang and other small birds hunted insects, enjoying the gently swaying foliage and the dappled sunlight that filtered through the leaves.

It was as they were passing a small inlet carved out by the river that Tim called out, 'Hey, stop punting a moment, Hugh. There's something odd in there.'

Hugh was in his stride, with an easy rhythm to his punting, and was not in the mood to stop. 'What is it?'

'Dunno. Looked like a white parcel, or a bag.'

'We'll look at it on the way back. Let's get on to the next bridge, it's not far now.'

Tim was a mass of doubt and indecision. There was definitely something unusual under the bank. Why couldn't he be more forceful and make Hugh stop? But there was probably a simple explanation. The river often washed strange things downstream after prolonged rainfall or flooding in winter; he had even seen a dead sheep once. Tim held his tongue.

Hugh was in high spirits, alternately humming to himself and whistling as he pushed the pole with easy movements into the water. Each stroke produced a cloud of mud and a spurt of bubbles that immediately washed away downstream. Meanwhile Tim brooded: what was that bulbous white mass under the willows?

Past the next bridge they drew alongside a small wooden jetty at the end of a long garden. They were in the old part of town now. 'Quick! Jump out and tie up as we touch,' called out Hugh. Tim grabbed the slimy rope, leapt from the front of the punt and wrapped it round a post. It took no more than a second or two, and then they were swinging gently with the current secured to the landing stage. Hugh relaxed and peered into the water, now flowing briskly over gravel. 'Some good uns here,' he said, watching two fair-sized chub and a grayling in the crystal-clear water. A van crossed the bridge behind them, and three town kids on the bank gesticulated and shouted out ruderies. A stern-looking woman in a tweed skirt walked purposefully down the garden towards them, which prompted Hugh to mutter under his breath, 'Silly old bag – I think we'd better move on.' Tim quickly jumped back into the punt and cast off as Hugh shouted out, 'Thank you, Madam. What a lovely day it is.' She folded her arms in reply.

Once away from the jetty they turned for home, at least an hour or two's journey but now with the current to help them. Back under the willow trees they sought out the mysterious 'package'. It had changed position somewhat; it seemed longer now and was on its side. A white foot rose to the surface.

'My God! It's a body!' The words squeezed themselves unbidden from Tim's mouth.

'Look! He's got no shoes or socks on, and he's only wearing shirt and trousers,' muttered Hugh, as he clutched at an overhanging branch to steady the punt. 'Poke at him with your pole, and roll him over so we can see his face.'

Tim was numb with shock and apprehension as he poked at the bloated and disfigured form. He felt faint and sick; he had never seen a dead body before, let alone one that had been in the water for some time. The grey and blotchy features of a young man finally appeared, surrounded by eddies of mud and wisps of weed. With a glutinous rolling motion the body turned itself face down again, its legs slowly sinking, the filthy white shirt partly filled with air, just as they had first seen it. The shocked boys looked at each other, not sure what to do next.

'We're miles from the farm,' said Hugh.

'My house is nearer. Just over those fields.' Tim was thinking hard. 'Perhaps I should go and tell Mum and she'll report it to the police.' He was anxious to get away from this grim place as fast as possible.

They were silent for a few moments, then Hugh said, 'Yes. I think that's best. Can you remember exactly where we are now?'

'I'll walk straight over to the path and tie my hanky to the fence as a marker.'

Tim was soon pushing his way through the trees and across the cowpat-covered field, not bothering about the stinging nettles brushing painfully against his legs. Never had he felt so pleased to escape from the river – yet this was his beloved place of retreat, where he came to renew his inner self, a haven of pleasure and relaxation. But for the moment this had

9. Tim and Hugh discover a dead body

cast a sinister shadow over his enjoyment. It was to be some time before he felt quite the same about the river again.

Several weeks later there was a knock at the door and a grim-faced Mrs Keeling took Mrs Mason into another room. They heard a sharp cry of anguish, followed by sobbing, as Mrs Keeling came back into the kitchen to say that their mother's father – Grandpa – had been killed in a terrible accident. She had taken the phone call from their Uncle John. 'Now, boys, you must be brave and not bother your mother. She's going to lie down and you mustn't disturb her.'

Later in the day, after more phone calls relayed through their next-door neighbour, the full story emerged. Grandpa Comber had retained the old family farm, with land on both sides of the railway line, and continued to run it with a skilled foreman and a skeleton wartime workforce. Meanwhile he had rented another farm some miles away, the one with regimental badges carved in the hillside, for his son John to farm. At supper, now recovered a little from the initial shock, Mother explained what had happened.

It was the foreman's day off, so Grandpa had carried out the regular chore of taking a few bales of hay over the level crossing to the small herd of store beef cattle in a field higher up on the farm.

'Is that the crossing with the friendly keeper?' asked Tim.

'Yes, that's the one. He told Grandpa that the 8.17 up train had gone through as usual but that the down train had been delayed by fog near London and was running half an hour late, and he would be telephoned when it was due. So he opened the gates, Grandpa crossed over with the tractor and the gates were shut behind him.'

'So now the line was clear for the other train to go through.' Tim struggled to keep up.

'Yes. The cattle were fine. Grandpa fed and watered them and returned to the crossing. Still the down train had not come and the mist, if anything, was getting thicker. Well, you know how impatient and grumpy Grandpa can be . . .' Tim started to snigger at this, but Chris cast him a withering look that made him stop instantly. 'So he got into a heated discussion with the crossing keeper and persuaded him against his better judgement to let him through. There had been no phone call so it seemed safe enough.' Their mother's voice faltered.

Annie, disturbed by all the talking, appeared from her bedroom rubbing her eyes. She climbed up onto her mother's lap. 'What's the matter, Mummy?' she asked, peering up into her face.

'Be quiet and listen,' said Tim, immediately ashamed of his gruff tone.

'Well, you know Grandpa was very deaf,' continued their mother, 'so when the gates were open he climbed onto his tractor and started crossing the lines just at the very moment that the train appeared fast round the corner. The sound of the tractor engine obscured the train's warning whistle and the crossing keeper's shout. Although it braked as hard as it could the train smashed through the gates, knocking Grandpa off his tractor – which then overturned on top of him.' Their mother choked back her tears as she carried Annie quickly back to bed. 'He was killed outright, crushed by the tractor.'

The boys sat in silence for some minutes. Chris finished his meal and went upstairs to his room; Tim pushed his plate aside and pondered. How would this affect their mother? Would she be sad and miserable, and not the cheerful old mum they had always known? She obviously loved her father, though she often said rude and critical things about him. And since he had died so suddenly would he have had time to say his prayers? Would he be allowed to go to heaven? There was a great deal to think about.

The complexities of life and the need to cope with them were making themselves increasingly apparent to Tim. Issues of life and death, brought to the fore by the body in the river and now Grandpa, were highlighted further some time later. There was a knock at the kitchen door, and from upstairs Tim heard what was clearly the start of a very serious conversation. He crept along the landing and peered through the knot-hole just as his mother put down a large basket of washing onto the kitchen

10. Grandpa is killed by a train

table. A neighbour was sitting out of his line of vision, but by her voice he recognised Mrs Price from opposite. She was clearly upset.

'Mary, I'm afraid the doctor thinks my Richard may have polio. He has a high fever and finds breathing difficult. He may have to go into hospital at very short notice.' Her voice trailed off and she blew her nose. 'The doctor's asked me to alert the parents of his immediate friends so they can watch out for similar symptoms.'

Mrs Mason felt a chill dread spreading over her. Richard often played with Tim; they were the same age, and Annie sometimes joined them.

Mrs Price continued. 'He was swimming in the river behind the Old Bell Hotel with some other boys and became ill later that evening. I dosed him up with codeine, but yesterday he was even worse. The doctor thinks he may have contracted polio from untreated sewage going straight into the river.'

The two women fell silent. Mrs Price sobbed and blew her nose again. Tim's mother could not bear the pleading look in her eyes and quickly turned away, saying comfortingly, 'I'm sure everything will turn out all right. It may just be a severe chill. I expect he'll be fine in a few days – you know how these things flare up in children. But thank you for coming to warn me. I'll keep a close eye on my two youngest for a few days.' After a cup of coffee Mrs Price left with red eyes and a bleak smile.

'Tim, come down, please. I need to have a word with you.'

At the kitchen table Annie was rolling out lumps of pastry, her hands and face covered in flour. She looked round at Tim, proudly pointing to a row of curly blobs ready for the oven.

'Who was that?' he asked, feigning innocence.

'I think you know already,' replied his mother slightly irritated; she was not in the mood for any silliness. 'Richard may have caught a very serious illness which can easily be passed on to other children, so we must be on our guard. I'm afraid you and Annie can't go over to the Prices' house any more till we're certain what the outcome is. In fact, I think it'll be better if you stay here at home for a few days and don't meet any of your friends, or go to their houses, till we know for sure they're not infectious.'

'It can't be that serious,' muttered Tim.

11. The boys observe the hearse from upstairs

'Yes, it most certainly can. This disease affects the muscles in your arms or legs and leaves them permanently withered. And if it attacks your chest muscles you can't breathe, and then you die. It's a terrible illness.'

'What about Chris? Doesn't he have to stay in too?'

'Chris's friends are much older and live further away. We're talking about the children who play with Richard, the younger ones who live in our street. They're the ones at immediate risk.'

Tim sulked at the thought of being stuck in the house and garden for who knew how long. 'It's not fair,' he muttered, stomping noisily upstairs.

The diagnosis was confirmed, and young Richard Price was taken away in an ambulance to hospital. For several days he fought for his life in an iron lung to assist his breathing, as all mothers in the street lived with an undercurrent of anxiety for their own children's safety.

Six days later Richard died, and shortly afterwards Mrs Mason appeared in the same black coat and little black hat with a pheasant tail wrapped round it that she wore after her father was killed. 'I have to go to the funeral now. Miss Brake will be round soon to keep an eye on you. Be good.'

'What's a fooleral?' asked Annie, but her question was ignored.

'Let's go upstairs and watch,' said Chris. They pushed the curtains in the upstairs bedroom gently aside as a group of sombre friends and neighbours climbed into three large black Wolseleys waiting outside the Prices' house. 'Well, you won't be playing with Richard any more, that's for certain,' said Chris softly.

13
BRIAN ENCOUNTERS A TANK AND LOSES HIS PARENTS

Everyone was talking about the long-awaited invasion of Europe. When would it take place and where? Surely it couldn't be far off now. Russia was driving the Germans steadily back, with terrible losses on both sides, after the turning-point at Stalingrad. Malta was no longer being bombed as the Allies forced their way through Sicily and Italy. The Italians had surrendered and the Nazis no longer occupied Greece.

Tim had noticed how full of military traffic the town was becoming, as line after line of lorries worked their way through the narrow medieval streets, drivers forced to stand up in their cabs at corners to heave the steering wheels round – there was no power assistance in those days! Night-times were becoming increasingly noisy; a background drone of heavy bombers interrupting their sleep as they crossed into France to destroy railways, marshalling yards and factories. During daylight hours the rasping growl of American fighter-bombers, passing overhead on their way to attack likely targets along the Channel coast, forced the boys to look up and wonder.

'Tell me more about the war,' demanded Tim, from his position at the end of the draining board as his mother shook soap flakes into the sink. Behind her a large galvanised-iron tub half full of water was boiling on the gas stove. It was early summer and the Beeston boiler, with its steel pipes that ran straight up through the kitchen ceiling to the airing cupboard above was not lit for three or four months to save fuel. And it was during this time that the old tin tub provided the family with its twice-weekly bath, little Annie first, then the others in turn, with a top-up of hot water in between. Annie loved her bath, sitting amongst the bubbles with her wooden ducks and boats, pouring water from bottle to bottle and generally splashing about. As much water went onto the floor as onto her, but that was half the fun of bath-night.

'Well, it was a war that had to be fought,' said his mother seriously. 'We're fighting for democracy against the forces of evil and darkness.' She uttered a short laugh at these pompous-sounding words, realising how easy it was to repeat phrases from the heroic figure of Winston Churchill. But by now she was in her stride. 'Hitler's rise to power came about partly because of the harsh settlement imposed on the German people at the end of World War One, and the misery and deprivation of the Great Depression that followed. Mind you, that affected the whole world, Europe and America as well as Germany, but Hitler used it to his advantage.'

'How did he do that?' asked Tim, keen that his mother should continue to unfold this fascinating historical drama.

'In several ways. He took control of the businesses and banks in his country, set the workers to building motorways, secretly drafted thousands into the navy and air force, and so put money back into the people's pockets. This gave them back their pride and made him a hero.' Tim pondered on all this, but each point seemed to lead to another. His mother felt he had had enough for one day. 'Why don't you go out and ride your bike?'

As Tim wandered aimlessly down the back steps he spotted Peter Keeling through a gap in the hedge. 'What are you up to?' he asked.

'Oh, nothing much. There are loads of lorries on the top road. Shall we go and have a look?'

This was something to do, so they pushed their bikes up the street, idly gossiping, and were soon joined by Brian Priddy. They could see that the volume of army vehicles was well above normal, with dozens of trucks full of American soldiers making their way towards the south coast. Usually they swept by at great speed, but if some sort of hold-up occurred they slowed down and occasionally stopped. This was an opportunity for the soldiers to laugh and joke with the boys, talking in their strange accents and throwing out goodies – chocolate bars, 'candies' (as they called sweets) and even Lucky Strike cigarettes. Then, like the body of some pulsating caterpillar, the column slowly moved off again, to bunch up when there was another hold-up.

Starting to lose interest in the lorries, the boys were about to cycle off when they detected a change in the sound of the traffic. After a steady hum of rubber tyres there was now a much deeper, thunderous, clanking sound. First of all a line of Bren-gun carriers streamed past, their tracks appearing to be almost alive as they flopped and writhed around the wheels. For Brian, this was an irresistible chance to throw stones at the armour-plated sides. They bounced off with a satisfying 'ping', but he knew he was safe as the drivers couldn't possibly stop, though they waved their fists and bellowed at him. As wider gaps occasionally developed between the vehicles he embarked on another dangerously stupid venture – playing 'chicken', dashing across the road on his bike in front of them and cutting back through the column when the next opportunity arose, always at the last possible moment.

'You idiot,' shouted Peter above the noise of the engines. 'You'll get yourself killed.'

During a lull in the almost endless convoy of vehicles, a black saloon car pulled up a little further along the main road and the driver went into a house. At the same time a cloud of blue-grey exhaust smoke seemed to envelop the entire road, accompanied by an even deeper roaring of diesel engines and the metallic thunder of tracks. A column of Sherman tanks had turned the corner at the top of the hill and was steadily bearing down on the watching boys. Brian, having taken advantage of this pause in the traffic to perfect a series of swooping curves on his bicycle in the middle of the road, looked up at the menacing forms of the tanks as they drew nearer and made a quick decision. At the very last moment he jumped on his bike to join the others.

The lead tank was forced, because of the parked car, to stop each track in turn to swerve round it. The manoeuvre was poorly executed. Almost certainly put off by Brian's stupid dash, the driver left the final correcting movement a little too late, and the tank careered up onto the pavement, shattering paving slabs under its tracks and spewing up gravel and earth. A look of pure terror appeared on his face as Brian tried desperately to yank the bike up out of the tank's way. In his agitation he lost his footing, the bike pedal caught on a kerbstone and it slipped sideways onto the road.

Brian let out a shriek of panic and fell in an untidy heap against the hedge. With a shattering roar and a blast of hot exhaust fumes many tons of heavy machinery slammed into the front wheel of the bike, instantly swallowing up its pedals and handlebars, and pulverising it into the wreckage of the pavement.

Conscious of his friend's shock, and his misery at having his bike wrecked, Tim instinctively put an arm round Brian's shoulder as they walked back home. After all, he was one of their buddies, and how was he going to explain the loss of his bike to his parents? He was surely in for a great deal of trouble.

It was not long before Tim was to appreciate more fully the significance of all this military traffic. As the boys were shaken awake by their mother on that momentous June morning to get ready for school, she said in an emotional voice, 'The Allies have landed in Normandy – the invasion's taken place at last. Perhaps soon this dreadful war will be over.'

At school the talk was of nothing else. Nearly all the boys had fathers or uncles fighting, and many of their mothers worked for the war effort. The headmaster's talk at assembly, normally ignored by the boys, was listened to attentively.

Throughout the day fighter-bombers flew overhead towards the beaches on strafing missions, the rasp of their engines ripping through the gusty squalls of rain and low cloud. During break-time two flights of three aircraft flew particularly low over the playground and wobbled their wings at the upturned faces. 'Whoopee! Thunderbolts. Off to smash Jerry tanks. Marvellous planes, tough as old boots!' Tim enthused loudly. He was in his element.

'Rubbish!' scoffed another boy, 'They're Typhoons!' Tim knew he was right, but was not prepared to argue.

On the following wet Saturday morning Tim stationed himself as usual at the end of draining board, holding a drying-up towel as Mother washed the breakfast things. 'It seems to have been a success,' she said, 'according to all the reports. The Allies have gained a solid foothold. Our

12. Brian's bicycle is crushed by a tank

casualties weren't too bad, thank God, though the Americans had a much worse time of it. Eisenhower seems to have pulled it off, and now we can only hope that Monty and Patton withstand the counter-attacks that are bound to follow.'

Tim bent down to pick up two forks he had dropped, and asked, 'What about the French? Are they helping?'

'Most certainly,' replied his mother. 'The French Resistance, who are called the Maquis, will be busy blowing up railway lines and knocking down telegraph poles to delay the arrival of German reinforcements.'

'Who are the Maquis?' asked Tim.

'They're French patriots, who object to their country being occupied by the enemy. Belonging to an enemy group is extremely risky, of course, and I imagine many have been imprisoned or shot already. I expect we're helping them in secret – but this is all very hush-hush, so we don't really know what's happening.' She shook a few more soda crystals into the lukewarm water and stifled a yawn with the back of her hand. 'And then there's General de Gaulle, leader of the Free French forces. He escaped to England with a number of French soldiers at the time of Dunkirk, and although he's a bit of a tricky customer in some ways Churchill realises his importance.'

Tim pondered all this new information but, sensing that his mother was getting tired of all his questions, decided not to pursue the matter.

The weather improved at last. One hot sunny morning, while Tim was feeding cabbage stalks to the rabbit, Brian Priddy poked his head round the corner of the house, hissed and beckoned. 'I'm staying with my aunt. My parents are away for a few days, visiting my uncle's pub in the country for a family get-together. It's their wedding anniversary, or something, and all the London relatives have come down for a long weekend. My aunt's too old to travel so she's looking after me. It's only for grown-ups – I wasn't invited.'

Tim wondered if there might be other reasons for not having Brian at the family do. He did seem to have the unfortunate knack of getting into scrapes and causing bother wherever he went.

Brian was riding his younger brother's bike, since his own had been crushed by the tank, and it was rather too small for him. But he didn't seem to care. 'Let's go and look at the glider that came down in the field above the main road last night.'

Chris was also interested, so the three pedalled off up the hill. Other boys had already pushed their way through the hedge surrounding the field, making tracks of flattened stalks in the as yet unharvested barley crop. A short way into the field lay the damaged glider, tipped over onto one wing, its back broken and its tail askew. The perspex nose had been kicked open to allow the crew to escape. Two white-helmeted military policemen were busy trying to keep a group of small boys away from the aircraft. Chris approached one of them and asked, 'What happened here?'

'It was on a night mission to drop commandoes behind enemy lines when something went wrong. Mind you, these pilots are really thrown in at the deep end with very little training. There's such a demand these days for glider assaults and not enough aircrew to man the planes. There's no sign of a broken towing cable, so I daresay the poor devil panicked and pulled the release handle by mistake. Go and have a look at it, but don't pinch anything.'

Tim ran his hand over the plywood structure of the cabin and marvelled at the soft floppy canvas, torn in several places, which stretched over the wings and tail. How amazingly fragile it all was. By peering through the escape door he could see the criss-cross aluminium struts that held the aircraft together. Could a dozen or more fully armed soldiers really fit inside this strange machine and be towed hundreds of miles to a foreign battlefield? He looked back at the long swathe of flattened barley, where the pilot had struggled to bring the glider safely down on its belly.

The policeman turned away from Chris to speak to the farmer who had just arrived, panting loudly and in a foul temper. It was Mr Tillman. The two brothers thought it best to remain hidden behind the tail as they listened to the angry exchanges between farmer and policeman.

'What's going on here? Can't you keep these people out of my field? They're wrecking my barley crop. It's bad enough having an aircraft tear up

13. *A glider makes a forced landing*

half the field without a load of flat-footed policemen stomping about – and now all these kids as well. When's it going to be removed?'

'That's very difficult to say,' said the policeman. 'The main priority is with our forces in Normandy. I'm afraid this isn't very important.'

'It is to me! I'm trying to feed the nation and now this happens. It really is the last straw.' The boys couldn't help sniggering at this unintended pun, but were glad when Mr Tillman's voice took on a gentler tone. 'No one hurt, I hope,' he said, indicating towards the glider.

'No, thank God. They got out all right. Just a few bumps and bruises, nothing serious.'

The boys chose this moment to show themselves, and returned to the road talking to Mr Tillman about the farm.

'About time you came and shot a few more rabbits,' he said to Chris. 'We're overrun at the moment.' He waved as he got into his battered farm truck and drove off.

Tim spent the rest of the day down at the river; Chris had gone elsewhere to be with his older friends. The usual activities kept Tim and Brian busy and amused for several hours – climbing trees, slipping and sliding in the mud, throwing stones at swans and running away, peering into birds' nests. They returned to Tim's house at tea-time, their trousers muddy and their shoes squelching with river-water. With enormous trepidation Tim asked, 'Mum . . . could Brian spend the night? His parents are away for the weekend and he's staying with his aunt, but he doesn't much like her.'

'She's an old bag!' exclaimed Brian, but blushed quickly and said, 'Sorry. I didn't mean to say that.'

'I should think not,' scolded Mrs Mason, hiding her face behind her hand to conceal her amusement. 'Just this once will be all right if your aunt agrees, since Chris is away for the night and his bed is free. Now behave yourselves and get out of those wet things while I make the tea.' Tim and Brian glanced at each other with secret pleasure and dashed upstairs.

A friendship had slowly developed over the last year or so, which had seemed to be of benefit to Tim. Mrs Mason, apprehensive at first, had noticed how Brian's lively, extrovert personality was helping to draw Tim out of his natural reserve. She hoped that some of the better qualities of each child might rub off on the other, to the benefit of both. Her good nature and strong Christian principles had softened her attitude to this unfortunate and possibly unloved child, who always managed to upset people by his bad behaviour; she was beginning to see him not as intrinsically naughty but more a victim of circumstances. She noted with pleasure that the two boys played together constructively that night, even involving Annie in their card games before her bedtime. Tim taught Brian the basics of chess and they finished off a jig-saw puzzle.

It wasn't till just after lunch the next day that the reality of the war hit them cruelly. They had fed the rabbit and guinea pig with carrots and had made their way up the garden to climb an apple tree. From high up in the branches they watched a car pull up outside. Surprised, they watched Brian's aunt, accompanied by a neighbour and a policeman, get out and go into the house.

'We're sorry to disturb you, Mrs Mason,' said the policeman, 'but a terrible thing happened during the night. One of those filthy doodlebugs must have fallen short or gone off course, and it demolished the Priddys' pub, just as the anniversary celebrations were coming to a close. I regret to tell you that Brian's mother, father and uncle have been killed. Some of the locals were amongst the casualties as well.'

Brian's aunt was visibly distraught, and dabbed her eyes with a handkerchief. 'It really is ironic. The relatives from London were looking forward to a quiet country weekend away from those dreadful V1s, which are causing such havoc up there at present.' Her voice faltered.

The policeman continued. 'Those flying bombs are notoriously unreliable, since many are sabotaged by the poor devils who are forced to build them. This one was probably on its way to Bristol, and since there are no reports of night-fighters in the area it can't have been shot down . . . it's just a terrible accident.' He shuffled his feet awkwardly, not sure what to say now that his unpleasant task had been completed.

A silence followed as Mrs Mason thought hard. She could see the boys struggling down from the lower branches of the apple tree, keen to find out the reason for this unexpected visit. 'Would you like Brian to stay for another night?' she asked. 'I can get him off to school tomorrow, if he feels like going.'

His aunt, sniffing into her handkerchief, pleaded, 'I don't think I can face Brian now. Could you possibly . . .?'

'Yes, of course, I'll tell him what's happened.' Brian's aunt gave a wan smile of thanks, and with a quick wave of her hand got back into the car.

Shaken, Mrs Mason sat at the kitchen table and considered what best to do. She felt real compassion for this unfortunate boy who was coping with friction in his own family and feelings of rejection. And now this. What a dreadful hand life had dealt him, the poor little soul.

At teatime Brian avoided asking about his aunt's visit, since he was enjoying himself so much and did not want to spoil things with what he guessed was probably bad news. Glancing up quickly, he asked, 'Tim suggested I could stay for another night. I can call in for my school things at my aunt's first thing in the morning. Is that OK?' His blushes and quick glance at the floor rather gave him away, and Tim was flabbergasted at his audacity, though secretly full of admiration. What a nerve he had!

Tim's mother thought quickly; this would provide a more suitable opportunity to break the terrible news, later on when he was ready for bed. She put her hand lightly on Brian's shoulder and said, 'Of course, dear.'

Another evening passed happily in the bedroom upstairs, though the scampering of feet and the creaking of floor boards indicated that a pillow-fight was taking place at one point. Finally the boys were called down for cocoa and a sandwich and told to get into their pyjamas. The moment that Tim's mother was dreading had finally arrived as she tucked them in and gave each a quick kiss on the forehead.

'Now, Brian, you have to be very brave. Your aunt brought terrible news this afternoon. I am afraid both your parents were killed by a flying bomb last night, during the celebrations at your uncle's pub. It was a direct hit and very sudden, so nobody suffered at all. It was over in an instant.'

Tim listened to his mother with a shocked expression, hardly able to believe what he was hearing. She was sitting on Brian's bed quite close to him as he suddenly sat up and threw his arms spontaneously round her neck. 'I guessed it was something like that,' he gasped. 'I just didn't want to know for sure. It's spoiled everything.' Collapsing back with a muffled

14. A flying bomb destroys the Royal Oak

sob, he burrowed under the bedclothes and pulled the pillow over his head. Time seemed to stand still as the three figures remained motionless and silent. After several minutes Mrs Mason slipped quietly out of the bedroom, leaving the door slightly ajar. Only then did she hear a series of suppressed sobs as Brian finally gave vent to his feelings of loss and despair.

14
TOBOGGAN RIDES AND TRAINS IN THE ATTIC

The long summer passed as the Allies pushed their way doggedly across France, Montgomery in the north and Patton further south. Paris was vacated by the Germans largely untouched and the privilege of leading the first Allied troops up the Champs-Elysées to the Arc de Triomphe was granted to General de Gaulle and the Free French Forces. It seemed that the war might be over by Christmas, but there was still the mighty River Rhine to cross.

Mrs Keeling stuck her head over the hedge one morning and said, 'Mary, come and look at this.' In the distance dozens of Dakotas and Halifaxes were pulling gliders across a clear blue sky. They were to learn later that these were reinforcements in aid of the Arnhem landings, which had taken place two days earlier in an attempt to capture a bridge intact across the Rhine – action that was shown later to be both unsuccessful and costly.

'It looks as though Patton will be the first into Germany,' laughed Mrs Mason. 'Monty will be livid. There's no love lost between those two!'

The winter that followed proved to be a hard one. Brian spent more and more time at the Mason household, now that he was living close by at his aunt's, and often brought his younger sister, Susie, to play with Annie, while Chris became more involved with his older friends. Tim watched him with mocking scorn – tinged with a little envy – as he pressed his long dark trousers with a damp cloth on the kitchen table until the creases were razor-sharp. He bathed more often and started shaving, leaving the house smelling heavily of deodorant. Tim ribbed him about these newly acquired rituals as much as he dared, sometimes risking such comments as 'And for goodness sake don't wake the entire household when you get back in the middle of the night. Some of us are still trying to sleep.'

The Germans counter-attacked in the Ardennes at Christmas-time in foul weather, with snow, heavy frosts and freezing fog covering most of northern Europe. 'Well, that's put an end to any hope of a quick end to the war,' their mother said. Coal, already rationed, was hard to get and the house got colder and colder. Only the sitting room was warmed with a fire in the evenings.

'Mr Moore said that if the snow lasted till the weekend he'd get out their large toboggan,' Chris informed everyone at breakfast one bitter Saturday morning. 'It's enormous and can take at least six people. We're going up to the old drover's track on the downs near the chalk-pit. There are always crowds of people there.'

'Good-oh!' said Tim, bursting with enthusiasm. 'I'll get our two sledges out of the shed – and we'll call in at Brian's on the way.'

'You'd better wrap up properly in jerkins and balaclavas – and don't forget scarves and gloves. I'll cut some sandwiches. Could you see if Suzie can come up and play with Annie for the day? Your sister's too young to get mixed up with all those town kids – she'll just get in your way.' Unfortunately this was the moment that Annie chose to walk back into the kitchen, overhearing these last remarks from her mother. An inevitable tantrum and floods of tears put something of a dampener on the day's plans.

At the Moores' house they helped slide the magnificent toboggan with its curved metal runners, wooden seats and hand-rails off the rafters in the garage and into the back of the estate car. Rather shamefacedly, Tim tucked the two little sledges built by their father some years earlier beside it. A few minutes drive over roads covered with black ice and hoar frost took them to the nearby hillside, where over the course of centuries the wheels of carts bringing crops down from the fields had cut deep sunken tracks. Almost all the children from the town appeared to be there, with a handful of accompanying adults. Small urchins with tin trays, youths with home-made sledges, young couples with smartly turned-out toboggans, and even the occasional older person on skis had gathered there in the weak sunshine and bracing air.

The night's snowfall had left a gentle covering on the hillside, which appealed to the youngest children and their parents. They enjoyed themselves throwing snowballs and building snowmen. In the deep sunken lane the snow had compacted into a fearsome sheet of ice, and it was here that the more reckless boys were rocketing down at breakneck speed towards the bramble and thorn hedge at the bottom. Several gaps had been forged through this natural barrier over the years, and the aim was to steer through one of these and then to pull up before hitting the barbed-wire fence at the end of the field beyond. The more expert tobogganers made it through successfully, but some did not – the more adroit of whom executed a quick roll off their sledge and, with arms and legs flailing the air, crashed into the frozen hedge in a shower of snow and icicles.

Mr Moore and his son John, assisted by Chris, dragged the heavy toboggan up to the top of the hill, as the younger ones trudged along behind, pulling their smaller sledges and looking with some trepidation at the route back down. At the top the toboggan attracted a crowd of curious boys.

'I think we'd better give it a trial run with just the three of us,' advised Mr Moore, as John and Chris climbed aboard and gripped the hand-rails. Tim and Brian exchanged a quick glance of nervous relief – their ordeal was postponed for a few more moments. Many willing hands pushed the toboggan to the crest of the run, keen to see it off on its maiden trip. Some of the town kids were a little too energetic in their assistance, secretly hoping that these 'posh people' with their flashy machine might come unstuck on the hazardous journey to the bottom.

The toboggan started sedately enough but quickly gathered speed. By half-way down it was careering from side to side with a rhythmic cracking of the compacted ice under its runners, its passengers jolted and shaken by the relentless vibration. By the time it reached the gaps in the hedge it was flying along in a barely controlled dash towards the barbed-wire fence, where it swung sideways with a jerk and drifted to a halt in the deep snow.

Once the sledge was back at the top again, the younger boys were called forward and nervously climbed aboard. Mr Moore sat firmly at the back gripping the rope, with Tim wedged between his knees and the others in front. 'Scared, are we?' jeered a scruffy lad as four pairs of hands

15. Mr Moore's toboggan sets off at speed

pushed them unceremoniously over the threshold of the run. Brian flung out an arm and clouted him behind the ear, which resulted in a string of obscenities. 'I'll get you for that!' he shouted, throwing himself headlong onto his homemade sledge and tearing past them in the first few yards.

The big toboggan's runners bit sharply into the ice with the added weight, but once momentum had built up the extra load increased their speed. The jolting and juddering was fierce and produced a sense of inevitability; nothing could stop them now. Tim's brain and stomach were taking a severe battering. He fought back a feeling of panic as a flurry of wind-blown snow hit him in the face, adding to the discomfort of the ice-cold air that was already buffeting him. He fixed his eyes on the hedge as it got rapidly closer, and wondered if they would find a gap to rush through. At that very moment Mr Moore pulled his leg out of the toboggan and ground the heel of his boot into the ice, causing it to make a graceful turn towards a gap. With a feeling of exhilaration mixed with relief, they came slowly to a halt.

'You'd better come indoors and warm up – we'll get a brew going.' Mr Moore stopped the car outside his front door and led Tim and Brian, shivering and grey-faced, into the house while John and Chris unloaded the toboggan and stowed it away in the garage. The sun was already setting and a dark, cold winter's evening stretched before them.

'Let's get those wet coats off you,' said Mrs Moore in a motherly way, undoing their buttons. 'Well, did you have fun?'

'Y-y-yes th-thanks,' stuttered Tim, his teeth chattering. 'It was really exciting but a bit scary on the big toboggan.'

'I expect you took it all in your stride, a couple of tough lads like you!' laughed Mrs Moore, turning towards the kitchen to get on with the tea. 'I've just rung Mrs Keeling to let your mother know you'll be back later if you'd like to stay on for a bit.'

Mr Moore helped them pull off their boots and put them next to the radiator to dry out. At tea Tim marvelled at the spread laid out for them: sandwiches, cakes, chocolate biscuits. This was nothing like home, where the rule was plain bread and butter first, then jam, and hardly ever cake or biscuits.

After tea John led Tim and Brian upstairs and pushed them into his bedroom. 'There are loads of things to do,' he said. The visitors looked around them in amazement at the Aladdin's cave of costly toys, some piled up in the corners, some half-made on the floor and under the bed. Tim lovingly picked up a large racing car with batteries and a starting lever; Brian was drawn to a Hurricane fighter made out of balsa wood. By the wardrobe was a model of an Indian fort made from coloured artificial stone blocks, complete with arches, steps, minarets and battlements.

Brian pulled out a tall crane with a wind-up motor, rope and hook, bolted together from strips of red and green metal. 'What the devil's this?' he asked abruptly.

'Gosh – it's Meccano,' replied Tim. 'You can build anything you like with it – look at all the illustrations in the booklet. There must be a box of nuts and bolts somewhere. Wow!'

Time passed. The friends discussed what to make, then lost themselves in concentrated activity as they busily joined sections together, arguing over which bit should go where. A hybrid vehicle slowly emerged, a mixture of lorry, tractor and tank.

'There aren't enough wheels. It'll look stupid.'

'No it won't. It can be a three-wheeler.'

They thought for a few moments, then scrabbled about in the box for more parts. A spare motor was put over the front wheel and connected up. 'There you are – problem solved!'

They laughed as the ugly, cumbersome, top-heavy juggernaut crawled slowly across the floor. The cat, which had just poked its head round the door, arched its back, hissed and rushed downstairs.

Some time later, though there was no guessing how long, Tim and Brian became aware of muffled voices and footsteps coming from overhead. Stepping out onto the landing they were intrigued to find their way blocked by a ladder which led up to a square of light. Cautiously climbing up, Tim peered over the rim and was amazed at what he saw.

The roof-space of the house was dominated by a rough brick chimney-breast covered in cobwebs. Dusty wooden rafters spanned the underside of the roof; dark grey-brown tiles ran from floor to ridge. As he looked around eddies of cold, dank air forced their way between cracks in the tiles and wafted over his face. Tim shivered, and beckoned Brian to follow him.

A pair of grey-stockinged feet nearly kicked him as he raised his head higher and stepped off the ladder. He could see a level surface of trestles and tables stretched around the chimney and away into the darkest corners of the loft. Moths, attracted to the three electric light bulbs that hung down from hooks in the rafters, cast flickering shadows over the extraordinary scene below. For there, in perfect proportion, lay a whole countryside in miniature: hills, woods and fields, houses and a church, a duck pond with ducks, the whole populated with tiny people. Weaving its way amongst this landscape was an entire network of railway lines, complete with points, signals, bridges and sidings with buffers. Waiting outside a station was a single-decker Dinky Toy bus; at the adjoining farm stood a tractor and trailer loaded with milk churns; a fire-engine was parked nearby, close to a group of cottages.

Two trains were flashing round the tracks. One, an express with maroon carriages, was being operated by John Moore, who by deftly twisting knobs on his control-box was able to slow it down round corners and stop it at stations. Chris was not so experienced, and his little green tank engine, pulling cattle wagons and a guard's van, had spun off at a sharp bend. Tim watched enthralled but did not dare interrupt at first. 'How does it all work?' he asked finally, unable to quell his curiosity.

'It's too difficult for you to understand,' muttered Chris angrily, annoyed that Tim had witnessed his engine coming off the tracks.

John Moore, always more tolerant and just a little amused at Chris's irritation, explained. 'The mains electricity comes up from downstairs and splits into three to go to the transformers and control boxes.' He was proud of his layout and more than happy to explain the technicalities.

'And since you haven't got a clue about transformers,' butted in Chris contemptuously, 'they convert the mains electricity from alternating

16. The boys play with trains in the attic

to direct current and reduce power at the same time. Not that you'll be any the wiser now!'

John laughed at the two boys bickering. He was an only child and missed having brothers. 'Tim, come and have a go with the third engine. It's in the tunnel at the moment behind the chimney. The control-box is by the station. Just put the switch to 'on' and turn the knob slowly clockwise. You'll soon get the hang of it.'

Brian had joined Tim by now, and together they manipulated the controls. Time seemed to stand still as they lost themselves in this Lilliput world of railways; of trains that backed in and out of tunnels, that stopped at stations, that carried cows and sheep in trucks and shunted them obediently into sidings.

Eventually it was time to stop and go home. Chris was staying the night at the Moores' house as he was going to a party with them, so Tim and Brian walked back together through the crisp darkness of a winter's night. They were accompanied by the mournful cries of owls as their feet scrunched on the rime already forming on the edges of puddles. Ridges of snow in the middle of the roads were rock hard and hurt their feet when they kicked at them.

When Mrs Mason went upstairs later to say goodnight the exhausted pair were fast asleep.

15
AN AIRFIELD ENCOUNTER AND UNWELCOME NEWS

'You're in luck,' announced Mrs Mason at breakfast, after Tim and Brian had slept in for at least an extra hour. 'Mrs Johnson rang the Keelings earlier to say that she's taking the canteen van up to the American airbase this morning. You can go with her to keep Philip company if you're there before ten o'clock.'

'Whoopee!' shouted Tim. He loved looking at the various types of aircraft and watching them being serviced, ready for another raid on Nazi-controlled territory. 'OK with you, Brian? You don't have to do much. Just tag along!'

They cycled down the road in high spirits. Mrs Johnson, an American woman married to an English army officer serving abroad, was in her volunteer's uniform, and was busy loading boxes of bread rolls and cakes into the khaki-coloured van. The letters YMCA in a dark red triangle were painted on the sides. Philip was filling a water tank inside the van from a hose-pipe sticking out through the kitchen window. 'Don't forget the milk bottles,' she reminded him.

Tim asked how they could help.

'Give Phil a hand with the food from the fridge, will you?'

Tim's eyes widened. He thought only butchers and grocers had refrigerated compartments, not ordinary households as well. They helped load milk, margarine, eggs, bacon and sausages into the cool boxes on the kitchen table and brought them out to the van.

'All ready, then?' asked Mrs Johnson, smiling. Let's be on our way.'

Crushed onto the front bench seat, the three boys watched the springtime countryside pass the windows. Mrs Johnson was a fast driver and not yet used to the narrow lanes of England. Snowdrops had now given way to early daffodils and the first leaves of the year were casting a pale green blush over the thorn hedges along the roadsides. Pink blossom was already blowing from the flowering cherries that grew next to the airfield gates.

'Howdy, Lizzie, and how are you this fine day?' asked the white-helmeted sergeant as he hitched his rifle higher onto his shoulder and peered into the cab. 'And what's this you've got here? Bit young to sign on as aircrew, aren't they? How many flying hours have they clocked up between them?' Mrs Johnson laughed as she was waved through.

This was the bit Tim really looked forward to. He cast his eyes round at the long concrete runways that seemed to stretch endlessly over the horizon, at the green and brown painted hangars, and at the Flying Fortress bombers, the sun glinting off their perspex noses and silver uncamouflaged wings.

In front of a row of hangars Mrs Johnson stopped the van, lit the gas stove, put on a large kettle and got the boys to wipe margarine onto bread for sandwiches. She got mugs ready for coffee and opened up packs of bacon and sausages. Soon, the water was boiling and the griddle plate hot. 'Better open up and wait for the rush,' she said, hooking up the long side panel and giving the horn a couple of toots. Men in khaki overalls converged on the van, laughing and joking as they came, wiping their hands on oily rags.

'Three coffees, please, Liz, and plenty of sugar. Not that you would need any in yours – you're that sweet already!'

'Well, thank you, kind sir, she laughed in reply.

'A fried egg butty and a coffee,' shouted another, loudly. 'My, Liz, you *do* look cute today,' he grinned at her in a playfully lustful way.

'That's a shame, Jack: you look just as ugly as you did yesterday.'

The waiting mechanics laughed at this and started hitting the popular loudmouth with their caps.

'Wally's half in a daze,' called out the next customer.' He's going stateside later this week on compassionate grounds. His wife's not too well.'

'I'm very sorry to hear about your wife, but I know you'll be pleased to see her,' said Mrs Johnson sympathetically. 'And to be home again.'

'They tell me the war's nearly over,' said an older man, taking off his cap and scratching at a balding head, 'now the Allies have crossed the Rhine. It can't last much longer, surely.'

'There's still time for our aircrews to get the chop,' replied another mechanic. 'You should thank your lucky stars you're too old to fly. Just keep stripping the threads on those engine changes and let the other poor beggars take the consequences!'

Mrs Johnson enjoyed the banter with her fellow countrymen; they seemed so full of spirit and energy in spite of the many months and years they had been in England servicing the bombers of the 'Mighty Eighth'. She knew how much they hated the British climate and how anxious they were to see their wives and families again. She was also aware that many of the unattached men had formed liaisons with English girls, and that in a short while these 'GI brides' would be taking the enormous step of accompanying their boyfriends and husbands across the Atlantic to start a new life in America.

As Tim ran up the steps to the back door, bursting to tell his mother all about his day, his excitement was dampened by the sight of Mrs Keeling sitting at the kitchen table, reading from a letter she had received that morning. It was from her husband who had recently advanced into Germany with his medical team. 'They seem to have discovered some ghastly things,' she was saying. Chris, hearing the two women talking, had come down from upstairs to join in.

Mrs Mason was nodding. 'And we're hearing exactly the same from my brother Pat. His regiment was one of the first to go into a sort of camp at a place called Belsen.' She hesitated for a moment, but then said firmly, 'I think you should both know about these things. It's exactly why we've been fighting this dreadful war and why the evils of fascism must be defeated.' She drew a deep breath and continued. 'Although the camp's not far from Munich it's been kept secret from the local population. They found hundreds of corpses lying around in heaps, unburied, and many more prisoners dying of starvation and typhus in the huts. There wasn't enough food because the German army was retreating, and only the guards were able to eat properly.'

Tim listened in shocked silence. Chris asked, 'What had the people been locked up for?'

'Apparently they were mostly political prisoners or common criminals, but there were also Jews and some foreigners.'

'And what seems almost unbelievable,' added Mrs Keeling, 'is that the Russians have overrun a vast camp in southern Poland where it looks as if possibly millions of Jews have been gassed over the last few years, with their bodies disposed of in furnaces. Some people are saying the Pope knew all about this, but wouldn't back any Allied attempt to deal with it.'

'Ah, but don't forget, Dorothy, the Pope lives in Italy – which under Mussolini was an ally of Germany. It's hard to see what he could have done in the circumstances.'

The adults paused for a moment as Chris asked logically, 'With the German armies so successful, what could the British or Americans do anyway?'

They were all forced to agree before his mother continued. 'And it's put paid to Pat's military career. He was so sickened by what he saw that he and two other young officers "borrowed" a jeep and drove to Paris for an unofficial weekend break. It caused the devil of a rumpus, and he's waiting to hear if there's going to be a court martial or not. Typical Pat – much too impetuous and always on the look-out for a bit of fun!'

'I'd better be getting back to sort out David and Peter's bedrooms,' said Mrs Keeling. 'They're coming back tomorrow for the Easter holidays. It's funny, really. The school was evacuated from London to Hemel Hempstead during the blitz in 1940 and was due to go back there once the danger was over. But what with one thing and another the move kept getting put off. Then the flying-bombs and rockets started during the summer, so the school stayed put in Hertfordshire.'

✼ ✼ ✼

Tim had learnt so much about the war during these last months from his mother that it was developing into a deep interest. A fascination with the hardware of war was also growing as he experienced at first hand the vehicles, guns and aircraft. The trip out with Mrs Johnson added enormously to his factual knowledge about bombers and the daily life of an airbase, but it also fed richly into his imagination. Almost lovingly he watched the lines of bomb trolleys being pulled by tractors from the half-buried bomb stores to the waiting Flying Fortresses. He could almost smell the mixture of oil, rubber and cordite inside the aircraft as the empty shell cases piled up under the waist-gunners.

But Tim was still to hear something that would soon intrude heavily upon both his imagination and dramatically affect his sense of reality. His mother was struggling to find the right time and manner in which to tell her sons and daughter that their father was presumed dead in an air accident in Burma. The Dakota aircraft in which he had been a passenger had been lost during a violent tropical storm some days earlier.

16
PEACE AT LAST

'Thank God it's all over,' said their mother in a weary but relieved voice, as Tim came downstairs rubbing the sleep out of his eyes. No longer did he squat on the third stair to peer secretly into the kitchen through the knot-hole; that period of his life was over now.

It was official. During Monday it had been announced on the wireless that the declaration of unconditional surrender had been signed. Hitler had been dead for over a week, while his immediate entourage had either been captured or had fled Berlin secretly. Goebbels and his wife had administered cyanide pills to their four daughters before shooting themselves. And all this with the Russians barely half a mile away from the Führer's bunker.

'Mr Churchill has declared today as VE Day, and a national holiday – and the King will speak to the nation on the wireless this morning. And guess what! All schools are shut for two days so everyone can enjoy the celebrations properly.'

'They're already building a bonfire down on the playing fields,' said Chris, who had been out earlier on his bicycle.

'So why not go and help them?' suggested his mother.

'No wood,' muttered a disconsolate Tim.

'Well, I'll tell you what!' she continued, thinking fast on her feet as ever. 'I'm sick and tired of that dreadful old coal shed. It leaks like a sieve and since those gales last winter it's been leaning at a crazy angle. You can't even shut the door these days.'

'Yes, it's completely rotten,' agreed Chris, 'but what'll we keep the coal in?'

'There's room in the wood shed for now, and during the summer holidays you and your fa . . .' She checked herself quickly, as Tim looked sharply at her. 'It'll be a nice little project for all you boys, including David next door, to build another. I'm sure you'll cope.'

'Well, I'm game. One push and it'll go over. What about you, Tim?'

Chris's enthusiasm was catching. 'OK. I'll go and get Brian.' He was feeling quite cheerful at the prospect.

Within half an hour the shed had been reduced to a pile of blackened timbers, sheets of rusty corrugated iron and broken window panes. Scratches from rusty nails and other cuts and grazes had been patched up with plasters, and the heap of wood was ready to be dragged down the road.

'We could load up the old pram, now Annie's much too grown up to need it. It'll be a much easier way to get it all down there.'

'Good idea,' said Mrs Mason. 'And then you can throw the pram on the bonfire as well. I never want to see it again – although, to be fair, it's seen plenty of action with the three of you!' Chris was about to make some quip about 'No more little Mason babies?' but thought better of it.

Many hands were already helping at the site of the bonfire. It seemed an ideal opportunity to get rid of cardboard boxes, bits of old furniture, broken fencing, old doors and windows, dead branches, old carpets, lino and mats, and even two brown left-over Christmas trees. In addition there were all those 'you never know when it might come in handy' articles that had been hoarded at times of acute shortage during the war years. The pile grew higher and higher. During the afternoon a lorry arrived with a dismantled bowling alley, some trestle tables and chairs, and two marquees. One was quickly established as a bar, with barrels of beer set up on a wooden stillage.

'I hope it'll settle before this evening,' grumbled a wizened farm labourer, casting a wary eye towards the arrangement. 'Don't worry,' said the driver. 'The beer's been filtered. It'll be fine.'

'Who cares what it tastes like?' said another old codger. 'It'll be the first peacetime pint for six whole years! As far as I'm concerned it will taste bloody marvellous!' They all laughed.

The evening was still young as the Mason and Keeling families wandered down the road towards the playing fields. 'They're lighting the bonfire at about eight o'clock, once it's dark,' said Tim, who had overheard one of the organisers earlier. 'And the hog-roast has been cooking all day so it should be lovely by now. Yummy! I can't wait.'

Brian met them later, in time to join the queue for a hog-roast roll. The greasy bits of pork and onion rings, dripping with tomato sauce, escaped infuriatingly through their fingers and fell onto the grass.

'Damn and blast,' muttered Brian, as a particularly juicy bit dropped next to his foot. He looked round quickly to see if anyone had heard his bad language as a small terrier slipped between his legs and bolted the morsel down. 'Get away, you little sod! That's my supper you're eating!'

'My word, you *have* done well with the bonfire,' said Mrs Keeling, casting an eye over the extraordinary objects buried inside. 'David and Peter have virtually cleaned out the garden shed. Sheila's old scooter and about ten rotten bicycle tyres were the first to go, then Leslie's old wooden trunk – the one he used to take abroad with him – and finally a completely bald set of tyres from the Morris Eight we sold last year.'

As the sun disappeared slowly behind the nearby downs the bonfire was doused liberally with paraffin and lit. This was the moment that all the small boys had been waiting for, their fire-raising instincts nurtured by six years of flame and destruction. They ran round it wildly, poked at it and pulled out burning sticks to use as swords. When they went too near they were scolded by their parents. A roll of old lino, softened by the heat, sagged at a rakish angle like the funnel of an Atlantic liner and puffed out a column of black smoke. At one point a car tyre, spitting flames, rolled out towards the crowd. It was at this point that two men dragged forward a lifelike effigy of Adolf Hitler, which they had hidden behind a hedge, and threw it on the fire. The crowd roared its approval as the sparks danced upwards into the sky like swarms of incandescent insects, temporarily obscuring the crystal whiteness of the stars.

At home Tim had often sat in darkness, gazing into the embers of the sitting room fire, creating images from their glowing shapes. Now, fascinated by the raw energy of this much larger fire, his imagination drew him back to a world so recently consumed in conflagration; to the burning carcases of crashed Lancaster bombers; to the firestorms of Hamburg and Dresden; to the flaming tanks of El Alamein and Normandy.

He felt a warm hand seeking his as Helen Borrodaile moved in close beside him, laying a cheek briefly on his shoulder. She smiled at him; and a turmoil of strange feelings overwhelmed him.

'Enjoying yourself? It's good fun isn't it?' She paused, waiting expectantly, then added, 'Why don't we move away and find somewhere quieter?'

He froze inwardly, feeling sick at his inability to respond naturally to his true feelings. Why was he so lacking in nerve, so emotionally inadequate? 'I think I'll just stay here and watch the fire,' was all he could finally blurt out. He hated himself as he said it, knowing that he was rejecting someone he had secretly thought about and longed for in a half-understood way. This was the moment when things might change for him dramatically – and he was throwing his chance away.

Helen did not withdraw her hand at once, and for a few magical moments they stood close together as time seemed to stand still. Then she slipped away into the darkness with a brief flourish of her dress.

In bed that night, as he relived ceaselessly those fleeting moments, he sensed that a new chapter in his life was about to start. Just as for the many people gathered around the bonfire that evening, there lay ahead an uncharted pathway of renewed life, of hope and promise.

www.ingramcontent.com/pod-product-compliance
Lightning Source LLC
LaVergne TN
LVHW081353060426
835510LV00013B/1808